VIOLENT EXTREMISM IN AMERICA

Interviews with Former Extremists and Their Families on Radicalization and Deradicalization

RYAN ANDREW BROWN ▪ TODD C. HELMUS
RAJEEV RAMCHAND ▪ ALINA I. PALIMARU
SARAH WEILANT ▪ ASHLEY L. RHOADES ▪ LIISA HIATT

Sponsored by the National Institute of Justice

For more information on this publication, visit www.rand.org/t/RRA1071-1

Library of Congress Cataloging-in-Publication Data is available for this publication.
ISBN: 978-1-9774-0679-8

Published by the RAND Corporation, Santa Monica, Calif.
© Copyright 2021 RAND Corporation
RAND® is a registered trademark.

Cover Images: AdobeStock/photolink; Azuzl
Cover Design: Peter Soriano

Support RAND
Make a tax-deductible charitable contribution at
www.rand.org/giving/contribute

www.rand.org

Preface

The January 6, 2021, attack at the U.S. Capitol, fueled by perceptions of a stolen 2020 presidential election, underscored a growing threat to America's national security: homegrown terrorism and ideologically inspired violence. Given this evolving, ongoing threat, the U.S. government, research institutions, and private-sector partners have made significant investments in attempting to understand and prevent violent extremism. Previous RAND work has described successes and failures of radicalization prevention programs. In this project, researchers at the RAND Justice Policy Program approached questions of extremist radicalization and deradicalization from a public health perspective. This report describes personal accounts from former white supremacists, Islamic extremists, and their family members about joining extremist groups and, in some cases, deradicalizing. This research was supported by the National Institute of Justice (Grant No. 2017-ZA-CX-0005).

Justice Policy Program

RAND Social and Economic Well-Being is a division of the RAND Corporation that seeks to actively improve the health and social and economic well-being of populations and communities throughout the world. This research was conducted in the Justice Policy Program within RAND Social and Economic Well-Being. The program focuses on such topics as access to justice, policing, corrections, drug policy, and court system reform, as well as other policy concerns pertaining to public safety and criminal and civil justice. For more information, email justicepolicy@rand.org.

Contents

Figures and Tables

Figures

Tables

Summary

The January 6, 2021, attack at the U.S. Capitol, fueled by perceptions of a stolen 2020 presidential election, underscored a growing threat to America's national security: homegrown terrorism and ideologically inspired violence. For some, as reports and images flooded social and traditional media, the assault might have come as a shock. But for many others, the incident was not surprising. Domestic attacks have maintained a steady and growing pace in recent years, and such events as the 2018 mass shooting at Tree of Life Synagogue in Pittsburgh, Pennsylvania, were grim foreshadowing of the latest incident.

Given this evolving, ongoing threat, the U.S. government, research institutions, and private-sector partners have made significant investments in attempting to understand and prevent violent extremism. What factors lead individuals to join violent extremist organizations? How and why do extremists become *deradicalized*, leaving their organizations, changing their minds, and in some cases joining the fight against radicalism? What can we do better to assist those who have been radicalized and prevent extremist organizations from recruiting new members? Efforts to answer such questions are closely tied to developing effective prevention and intervention measures.

Researchers from the RAND Corporation approached questions of extremist radicalization and deradicalization from a public health perspective. First, we looked at radicalization and its prevention at four levels—individual, relational, institutional, and societal. This multilevel approach is based on the U.S. Centers for Disease Control and Prevention's socioecological framework for violence prevention. Second, we adapted the psychological autopsy approach, used to understand suicide, to talk with individuals formerly involved in extremist organizations, as well as family and friends of former, current, or deceased members of extremist groups. These two methods, along with a close review of current literature, offered insights that can be considered by policymakers and community organizations working to develop antiextremist policies and practices, as well as by researchers who continue to look for answers.

Study Methods

The research team began by reviewing current studies focused on radicalized U.S. citizens residing in the United States. Most of the studies considered used primary-data collection through interviews, surveys, or other targeted data with radicalized or deradicalized individuals, their family members, or peers. The team also reviewed information contained in the Profiles of Individual Radicalization in the United States (PIRUS) database.

Using findings and insights from these sources, the team designed a semistructured interview protocol for former extremists, as well as their family members and friends. The structure of these interviews is based on the psychological autopsy approach, which involves systematic interviews with family and friends used to learn about a person who died by suicide and events leading up to the death. To recruit respondents, the team partnered with Parents for Peace and Beyond Barriers, two organizations that work with former members of radical extremist organizations and family members who have assisted with deradicalization efforts.

Through these efforts, the team was able to conduct 36 interviews: 24 former extremists, ten family members, and two friends. Together, these interviews covered 32 separate cases of radicalization and deradicalization. Of all 32 cases, 24 were white supremacists (eight females and 16 males), and eight were Islamic extremists (one female and seven males). Across all 32 cases, 17 were involved in extremist organizations in the 2000s, with six involved prior to 2000, and six across both eras (three did not provide this information). Sixteen individuals had *violent intent*, defined as engaging in or planning violent activities during their time in the organization. Seven of the focal individuals involved in these 32 cases were deceased, imprisoned, or otherwise unavailable for interviews; in these seven cases, interviews were conducted with friends or family members exclusively.

Most interviews were conducted via telephone. Five were conducted in person at an annual meeting for one of the partner organizations. To guide the interviews, participants were asked to begin by describing their (or their friends' or family members') early lives. They then were asked to describe major warning signs and turning points, any attempts to intervene, and processes of leaving the group and deradicalizing. Respondents were also asked to share ideas for intervention. The interviews were transcribed, deidentified, and systematically coded to produce key themes for analysis.

Study Findings

Together, the interviews presented findings in four key areas: background characteristics of radical extremists, pathways to radicalization, deradicalizing and leaving extremist organizations, and participant perspectives on mitigation strategies, summarized below.

Background Characteristics of Radical Extremists

Existing studies identify many factors that potentially contribute to radicalization. Individuals are made vulnerable by factors including social isolation, personal trauma, substance misuse issues, and more. Families also can influence the change: Family discord or lack of parental supervision or support are the two factors most cited. Finally, the literature describes several community, societal, and cultural factors that can influence radicalization. These include perceptions of discrimination or victimization, belief in the cause of an extremist group, living in underserved communities or those with elevated crime rates, and contact with recruiters or radicalized individuals.

The RAND interviews highlighted several factors that might have contributed to individuals becoming radicalized in this study:

- *Financial instability.* This factor was mentioned in 22 cases. Seven individuals noted financial challenges as a driver to their extremism. Financial challenges were also mentioned when people were in extremist organizations, causing some to work in jobs tied to the organization itself and leading to delays in leaving the organization.
- *Mental health.* This factor was mentioned in 17 of the 32 cases. Mental health challenges were cited as presenting obstacles throughout the individual's life. Some identified such symptoms as overwhelming anger as a driver of their joining extremist organizations. Trauma or posttraumatic stress disorder, substance use, and physical health issues were also mentioned, but less frequently.
- *Social factors.* Victimization, stigmatization, or marginalization was mentioned in 16 cases. Many interviewees described feeling one or more of these when growing up and that these experiences contributed to their radicalization. Most often, individuals mentioned feeling isolated and lonely in institutions (e.g., schools) or communities in which they were the minority race; former white supremacists cited this factor, as did one former Islamic extremist. Radical beliefs in the family were only infrequently mentioned.

Pathways to Radicalization

To date, current literature suggests that online propaganda and recruitment are important pathways toward radicalization. Criminal activity and imprisonment are also cited as prevalent paths.

Our interviews highlighted several pathways that played a key role in radicalizing individuals:

- *"Reorienting" event.* More than half of the 32 cases described a dramatic or trau-matic life event that prompted an individual to reconsider previously accepted views and reconsider alternative views and perspectives. These included a gun possession charge, rejection by the military, a friend's suicide, and an extended period of unemployment. For some white supremacists, the reorienting events involved black individuals.
- *Propaganda.* Twenty-two cases described consuming propaganda during radical-ization, including especially online materials but also music and books.
- *Direct and indirect recruitment.* Seven cases (four white supremacists and three Islamic extremists) involved top-down recruitment, in which recruiters from rad-ical organizations formally and proactively recruited them. Eighteen cases (15 white supremacist, three Islamic extremist) involved bottom-up entry, in which individuals radicalize on their own and then seek membership in extremist orga-nizations.
- *Social bonds.* Creating and forming social bonds was identified in 14 cases as a motivating factor for joining extremist groups. Several cases were identified in which individuals "graduated" from one organization to a more extreme organi-zation.

During the interviews, respondents also discussed positive experiences while par-ticipating in extremist groups. Most noted feelings of family and friendship. Others noted a new sense of power. As one study participant told the interviewers: "People switch the side of the street when they see you. . . . It was a great feeling." Some noted that they had felt they had a new mission in life, while others noted how they felt rewarded for contributions to the cause and group.

Among the 32 cases, many cited instances of an observable behavior change in the early stages of radicalization. Two Islamic extremists showed outward signs of reli-gious conversion; two others did not convert, but one became "extremely quiet" and the other "started wearing religious clothing associated with extreme Islam and voic-ing more-extreme ideas to family." Among white supremacist cases, interviewees noted how they began to create racist videos, use racial slurs, and display icons and symbols associated with white supremacy on their bedroom walls, clothing, and jewelry.

Deradicalizing and Leaving Extremist Organizations

Like radicalization, there is no standard model of how people turn away from or reject extremist views or why they leave extremist groups. Nonetheless, the existing literature does identify factors that *push* and *pull* members out of such beliefs and related alli-ances. Among those that push people away is a sense of disillusionment with the group or belief, an inability to maintain employment, feelings of burnout, and distrust. Pull factors include a diminished sense of security when a group of members leaves together.

Among the RAND sample, most (20 out of 32 cases) had exited a radical organization and had undergone a process of psychological and social deradicalization. Out of these 20 cases, most of them (12) were also activists, currently engaged in deradicalizing others. Six had exited a radical organization but were still undergoing cognitive and emotional deradicalization.

The most commonly mentioned factor for exiting a group in the RAND interviews were senses of *disillusionment and burnout*. These feelings were noted in 14 cases (13 white supremacists and one Islamic extremist). Specifically, these cases expressed feelings of disappointment by the former members; hypocrisy or other negative behaviors were cited as reasons for these feelings.

Help and Intervention to Exit

Individuals or groups helped 22 of the cases in the RAND sample exit extremist groups. Such actions were often conducted intentionally. Individuals who helped people exit these groups included acquaintances, life partners, other former radicals, friends, journalists, children, other family members, religious authorities, current radicals, therapists, or school officials. The interventions consisted of diverse cultural and demographic exposures, emotional support, and financial or domestic stability. Some cases highlighted noxious or negative impact from radical individuals, which could be described as an inadvertent intervention. In 11 cases, the intervention was orchestrated and conducted by an institution, including religious groups, law enforcement, and secular nonprofits. Twenty-two of our 32 cases also described processes of *self-driven exit* from extremism.

Failed Interventions

In 19 cases, interviewees indicated that they experienced interventions that failed. These cases most often involved family members who tried to intervene. Punitive interventions by law enforcement also often led to paradoxical effects of increased extremism. Upon leaving extremist organizations, six cases described feeling drawn back to organizations or ideologies. This was linked to missing the thrill and other psychological benefits of being involved in radical extremism, exacerbated by postexit social isolation and triggered by current events.

Participant Perspectives on Mitigation Strategies

There is currently a lack of rigorous evidence evaluating interventions for preventing radicalization or promoting deradicalization. Nonetheless, there are organizations working to identify individuals at risk of extremism and working to assist community members.

Interviewees were asked for ideas about preventing radicalization or promoting deradicalization. They offered several suggestions about each.

In terms of preventing radicalization, study participants noted the importance of childhood as a key time to be exposed to diverse ideas, develop critical thinking skills, participate in prosocial activities designed to promote positive behaviors and inclusive-ness, and be exposed to members of different racial or cultural groups. Interviewees also mentioned the need to address marginalization more broadly, as well as polariza-tion and media sensationalism. Also discussed was the need for better access to mental health treatment and targeted outreach and support for military veterans.

In terms of promoting deradicalization, study participants noted the need to reach extremists at the *right time and place.* They also made recommendations on who should deliver messages, how to provide social support, and how extremists should be engaged. Also, some respondents mentioned unplanned exposures to diversity and kindness, religious education, and mental health interventions. Many also criticized the criminal justice system's approach to radicalization. Finally, some interviewees dis-cussed the need to support families of extremists.

Conclusions and Recommendations

These analyses offer findings that may be useful in ongoing investigations of the pro-cesses by which people join and leave extremist organizations. That said, the study is limited in sample size, includes no comparable control group, and, like all studies based on interviews, may offer insights based on incorrect recollections. Nonetheless, the findings support recommendations for community policymakers and researchers who continue to work toward reversing the dangerous trends of homegrown terrorism and ideologically inspired violence.

The study findings and correlating recommendations for community organiza-tions and researchers working in the area are summarized in Table S.1.

Table S.1
Summary of Study Findings and Recommendations

Study Findings	Recommendations
Negative life events are part of, but not the sole cause of, radicalization. Abuse or trauma, difficult family situations, bullying, and other negative life events often have psychological and behavioral consequences and are sometimes implicated in radicalization pathways. However, they are never the sole or most direct cause of radicalization.	*Community organizations:* **Expand opportunities for mental health care.** Although it is not possible to establish the causal effect of mental illness on extremism, the plausibility may provide incentives to buttress mental health services in locales at high risk of extremist recruitment and activity. And targeting mental health care toward active extremist populations may provide an opportunity to directly support disengagement.
The enduring appeal of extremist groups seems to lie in attending to fundamental human needs. Social bonds, love and acceptance, and having a life purpose sometimes go unmet for some people, leaving them prone to become involved with extremist views and groups.	
Radical ideology and involvement in extremist activities have addictive properties for many. Physical violence and trading insults online have addictive properties that appear linked to the experience of joint risk and struggle.	*Researchers:* **Explore the feasibility of addiction-based programs to hate and radicalization.** Buddy systems can deter radicalization relapse. Such programs treat radical involvement as a lifelong struggle using a chronic disease model, which matches the subjective experiences of many study participants.
Recruitment to radical groups deliberately leverages personal vulnerabilities. Radical groups develop ways to bolster ideological commitment through (1) restriction of access to information or circumstances that challenge ideological constructs and (2) social and cognitive strategies for reinforcing in-group bias and hatred toward people outside the group.	*Community organizations:* **Provide opportunities for expanding diversity exposure.** Exposure to diverse populations played a critical role in helping to deradicalize and reorient a number of former extremists in the study. This suggests that diversity-exposure efforts could be more systematically exploited to limit the risk of radicalization or possibly deradicalize already extremist members.
	Researchers: **Better identify geographic and demographic hot spots for radicalization.** Not all communities are equally at risk of violent extremism. Interviewees in the study hinted that there are possible dangerous environments for radicalization, including poor rural environments with recent demographic and economic change, prisons, and high-density urban environments.

Table S.1—Continued

Study Findings	Recommendations
Extremist groups nurture a self-reinforcing social milieu. This includes shared purpose, camaraderie, friendship, and joint activities, all of which can involve both risk and emotional rewards.	*Community organizations:* **Help at-risk parents and families to recognize and react to signs of extremist radicalization and engagement.** Some signals, such as observing youth consuming extremist propaganda or wearing or showcasing extremist symbols and paraphernalia, serve as unambiguous signs of at least a dabbling interest in extremism.
	Researchers: **Explore and develop educational and outreach efforts to help recognize and address signs of radicalization.** The interviewees identified several early signs of radicalization that friends, family, and others are able to notice. Organizations made up of former radicals currently run help lines and other efforts to provide support to family members, friends, and others, as well as to provide them with tools to recognize potential signs of radicalization and suggestions for when, where, and how to (and not to) intervene.
	Researchers: **Explore and design social network approaches to deradicalization.** In the study, former extremists described how they used their own social connections to find and approach individuals in radical organizations who might be ready to leave these organizations and deradicalize.
Both radicalization and deradicalization can be triggered. An individual's experience of a dramatic, challenging life event, of being at the right place at the right time, can encourage both processes.	*Community organizations:* **Present deradicalization messages at the right time and place.** Advertisements and public service announcements about existing resources for individuals who want to deradicalize can be delivered by the right person in ways and through multiple media that reach those at the cusp of changing or who are likely to change.
	Researchers: Design and assess programs that create a safe, mentored space for individuals to freely express themselves and challenge one another's beliefs. Former radicals in the interviews described feeling marginalized and avoiding exposure to "mainstream" contexts after feeling stigmatized or targeted for their beliefs. This led some to further radicalization in "niche" information environments. This and other studies indicate that nonconfrontational challenges to incorrect beliefs are more productive than direct challenges.
	Researchers: **Continue to explore and design interventions that foster deliberate exposure to "optimal contact" with groups targeted by hatred.** Former extremists described strategic exposure to positive experiences with ethnic minorities or others whom radicals were taught to hate, creating sometimes transformative effect. However, there are conditions under which contact tends to lead to better outcomes and increasing recognition that cross-group friendship is especially important.

Table S.1—Continued

Study Findings	Recommendations
Heavy-handed attempts by formal institutions to deradicalize individuals often fail. Such measures taken by intelligence and law enforcement agencies are understandable because of the need to protect the public but can sometimes deepen ongoing radicalization processes and push potentially salvageable cases to more-extreme behaviors and involvement.	*Community organizations:* **Consider the trade-offs between punitive and "soft" law enforcement interventions.** Although interdiction of ongoing violent plots is an obvious target for traditional law enforcement responses, notification regarding the ongoing radicalization of individuals may warrant a different response *Researchers:* **Conduct research on institutional and societal (environmental) influences of extremism.** Public health and demographic research are increasingly examining how institutional and societal factors, such as unemployment, segregation, and income inequality, are associated and might produce certain health outcomes, including obesity, drug misuse, and suicide.
Stigmatization of groups seems mostly to push at-risk individuals further down the extremist path. Punitive measures, banned speech, and indignant public discourse can backfire and increase the drive for radicalization.	*Researchers:* **Design and assess programs that create a safe, mentored space for individuals to freely express themselves and challenge one another's beliefs.** Former radicals in the interviews described feeling marginalized and avoiding exposure to "mainstream" contexts after feeling stigmatized or targeted for their beliefs. This led some to further radicalization in "niche" information environments. This and other studies indicate that nonconfrontational challenges to incorrect beliefs are more productive than direct challenges.
Media literacy and open access to diverse sources of information appear critical for deradicalization. In certain cases, structured interventions that involve exposure to people outside the group who exhibit kindness and generosity seem to have positive effects.	*Community organizations:* **Organize community-based educational opportunities.** These can cultivate media literacy and responsible internet use. *Researchers:* **Use both data science and ethnographic research to understand current processes of online radicalization to extreme groups.** Most study respondents were exposed to extremist propaganda online. Creative use of online and offline interviewing and group observation is needed to further understand these radicalization processes and how best to disrupt them.

Acknowledgments

We are extremely grateful to all our participants for sharing their important stories. We are also very grateful to our partner organizations, Parents for Peace (led by Myrieme Nadri-Churchill) and Beyond Barriers (led by Jeff Schoep), for entrusting RAND with connections to their members and associates and for all the collaborative work throughout the project. We would also like to thank Katheryn Giglio for her communications expertise and our peer reviewers: Miriam Matthews at RAND and Amarnath Amarasingam at Queen's University.

Abbreviations

ADD	attention deficit disorder
ADHD	attention deficit hyperactivity disorder
CDC	Centers for Disease Control and Prevention
CVE	countering violent extremism
FBI	Federal Bureau of Investigation
HSPC	Human Subjects Protection Committee
ISIS	Islamic State of Iraq and Syria
KKK	Ku Klux Klan
NSM	National Socialist Movement
PIRUS	Profiles of Individual Radicalization in the United States
PTSD	posttraumatic stress disorder
TWP	Traditionalist Worker Party
YWC	Youth for Western Civilization

CHAPTER ONE

Introduction and Background

Violent Extremism in the United States

Despite years of counterterrorism operations and numerous countering violent extremism (CVE) initiatives, violent extremists touting a wide variety of ideological causes continue to plague the United States.

Violent Islamic extremist organizations, such as al Qaeda and the Islamic State, have captured American headlines since the attacks on September 11, 2001. Having planned and executed the 9/11 attacks, al Qaeda constituted a central terrorist threat to the United States and helped inspire such high-profile attacks the 2009 attack at Fort Hood, Texas, and the 2013 Boston Marathon bombing.

In 2014, the Islamic State of Iraq and Syria (ISIS) supplanted the homeland threat from al Qaeda. ISIS established a self-style caliphate in Iraq and Syria and inspired waves of foreign fighters to join its cause. Among these, 330 North Americans joined ISIS fighters in Syria. Others took inspiration to act at home in the United States. An attack in Orlando, Florida, killed 49, and an attack in San Bernardino, California, killed 14.[1]

Throughout this time, right-wing extremists, connected to a panoply of white supremacist and antigovernment organizations and ideologies, kept up a steady and growing pace of domestic attacks.[2] Since at least 1994, right-wing extremism accounted for the majority of terrorism plots and attacks in the United States, significantly outpacing those of Islamic extremism. And the rates have only grown. Seth Jones and colleagues, for example, document five right-wing plots and attacks in 2013, but that

---

[1] Donna Henderson-King, Eaaron Henderson-King, Bryan Bolea, Kurt Koches, and Amy Kauffman, "Seeking Understanding or Sending Bombs: Beliefs as Predictors of Responses to Terrorism," *Peace and Conflict*, Vol. 10, No. 1, 2004; Ahmed Kawser, "Radicalism Leading to Violent Extremism in Canada: A Multi-Level Analysis of Muslim Community and University Based Student Leaders' Perceptions and Experiences," *Journal for Deradicalization*, No. 6, Spring 2016.

[2] As we note later, *white supremacists* refers to those who espouse the belief that the white race is superior to and should exert control over other races.

number grew to 53 in 2017 and 44 in 2019.[3] These numbers are punctuated by the attack at the El Paso, Texas, Walmart that killed 23 and the attack at Tree of Life Synagogue in Pittsburgh, Pennsylvania, that killed 11.[4]

The January 6, 2021, attack at the U.S. Capitol, fueled by perceptions of a stolen 2020 presidential election, highlights a potentially worsening threat. Many right-wing extremist groups were already on the cusp of violence, and feelings of alienation and defiance may push them over the edge. As terrorism expert Brian Michael Jenkins notes, political leaders have already come under death threats, and a plot to kidnap a governor has been foiled: "It is not difficult to imagine . . . attempted assassinations of political leaders and other acts of terrorism."[5]

Given this evolving and ongoing threat, the U.S. government, research institutions, and private-sector partners have made significant investments in attempting to understand and prevent violent extremism. Between 2010 and 2018, the U.S. government invested more than $20 million into understanding radicalization to extremist violence, as well as effective prevention and intervention measures.[6] Efforts to understand radicalization are closely tied to developing effective prevention and intervention measures. Specifically, effective prevention efforts must ultimately be premised on a sound and scientific understanding of the pathways that life trajectories take that lead individuals to accept calls from violent extremist organizations and the methods, including propaganda and recruitment strategies that groups undertake to indoctrinate and acquire new members. By the same token, research on the deradicalization process informs intervention programs to help pull radicalized individuals out of extremist organizations and reintegrate them into society.

This report seeks to add to the growing body of literature that sheds light on the radicalization and deradicalization process. It does so by drawing on in-depth interviews with individuals who were formerly involved in extremist organizations and family and friends of former, current, or deceased members of extremist groups.

Definitions and Terms

Before describing the rationale for our research approach, our methods, and our results, we define up-front the terms that we will use **throughout** the report.

---

[3] Seth G. Jones, Catrina Doxsee, and Nicholas Harring, "The Escalating Terrorism Problem in the United States," Center for Strategic and International Studies, June 17, 2020.

[4] Briana Vargas and Joel Angel Juarez, "El Pasoans Remember Victims of the Walmart Shooting One Year Later," *Texas Tribune*, August 3, 2020; Campbell Robertson, Christopher Mele, and Sabrina Tavernise, "11 Killed in Synagogue Massacre; Suspect Charged with 29 Counts," *New York Times*, October 27, 2018.

[5] Brian Michael Jenkins, "The Battle of Capitol Hill," *RAND Blog*, January 11, 2021.

[6] U.S. Department of Homeland Security, "Snapshot: S&T Develops the First Line of Defense Against Acts of Targeted Violence," August 28, 2018.

- *Extremism* refers to fanaticism or the "holding of extreme political or religious views."[7]
- *Violent extremism* refers to the "encouraging, condoning, justifying, or supporting the commission of a **violent** act to achieve political, ideological, religious, social, or economic goals."[8]
- *Terrorism* is the "use of violence and intimidation, especially against civilians, in the pursuit of political aims."[9]
- *Radicalization* is "the action or process" leading someone to adopt "radical positions on political or social issues."[10]
- *Deradicalization* is "the process of changing an individual's belief system, rejecting the extremist ideology, and embracing mainstream values."[11]
- *White supremacist* or, alternatively, *white nationalist* groups espouse the belief that the white race is superior to and should exert control over other races.[12] Groups adhering to this ideology and commonly referenced in this document include the Ku Klux Klan (KKK), skinheads, neo-Nazis, American Nazi Party, Heritage Front, Hammerskin Nation, National Socialist Movement (NSM), and Traditionalist Worker Party (TWP).
- *Islamic extremist* refers to extremism associated with the Islamic religion. Relevant groups referenced in this report include al Qaeda, ISIS, and al Shabaab.

Rationale for the Current Approach

Research on radicalization and extremism has grown as rapidly as concerns about terrorism have increased, but the field remains beset by at least two key challenges. Two recent systematic reviews identified more than half of the studies in the field to be methodologically or empirically poor.[13] But perhaps more importantly, most research relies on secondary-data sources, most commonly historical archival research, to com-

---

[7]   Oxford University Press, "Definition of Extremism in English," Lexico.com, 2020a.

[8]   Federal Bureau of Investigation (FBI), "What Is Violent Extremism?" "Don't Be a Puppet" website, undated (emphasis added).

[9]   Oxford University Press, "Definition of Terrorism in English," Lexico.com, 2020c.

[10]   Oxford University Press, "Definition of Radicalization in English," Lexico.com, 2020b.

[11]   Bryan F. Bubolz and Pete Simi, "Leaving the World of Hate: Life-Course Transitions and Self-Change," *American Behavioral Scientist*, Vol. 59, No. 2, 2015.

[12]   *Merriam-Webster*, "White Supremacist," undated.

[13]   P. Neumann and S. Kleinmann, "How Rigorous Is Radicalization Research?" *Democracy and Security*, Vol. 9, No. 4, 2013; A. McGilloway, P. Ghosh, and K. Bhui, "A Systematic Review of Pathways to and Processes Associated with Radicalization and Extremism Amongst Muslims in Western Societies," *International Review of Psychiatry*, Vol. 27, No. 1, 2015.

pile and analyze case studies of radicalization. Thus, many recent studies have drawn from the same cases using nearly the exact same sources of data (news articles, court transcripts, and other publicly available data). The studies have used different hypotheses to drive data analysis but have been unable to bring in new sources of data or knowledge. In addition, these studies rely almost exclusively on secondhand or otherwise biased sources of data.[14] Media accounts may be uneven and biased toward collecting and disseminating scintillating information on subjects and fail to report information that may prove critically important to understanding the radicalization process. Journalist interviews with friends and family of terrorism suspects may be in-depth interviews, much less structured, and many take place very shortly after the terrorist incident.[15] Court documents, too, can be biased. It is the job of investigators and prosecutors alike to dig up incriminating information about the terrorism suspect, a process that can hardly be considered objective.

In September 2016, the National Academies of Sciences, Engineering, and Medicine convened a workshop titled "Exploring the Use of Health Approaches in Community-Level Strategies to Countering Violent Extremism and Radicalization," a goal of which was for the interdisciplinary audience, consisting of both researchers and practitioners, to consider health-centered approaches to CVE and radicalization. Formally, this included considering whether public health research methods could be applied to conduct formative research on radicalization, whether health-related evaluation designs could be used to evaluate interventions geared toward preventing radicalization, and whether evidence-based public health strategies could be applied in communities to prevent radicalization. This echoes commentary by Bhui and colleagues in which they stressed the need for public health approaches to inform population-based interventions to prevent violent radicalization.[16] They proposed a cyclical process whereby public health surveillance informs research into the causes and factors that increase risk and that can be modified, which thus informs intervention strategies that can then be implemented. However, as described above, surveillance systems that enable one to identify risk factors are lacking.

When proposing how public health methods can fill these gaps, Bhui and colleagues emphasized themes from the U.S. Centers for Disease Control and Prevention's (CDC's) socioecological framework for violence prevention (see Figure 1.1).[17]

---

[14] Bart Schuurman, "Research on Terrorism, 2007–2016: A Review of Data, Methods, and Authorship," *Terrorism and Political Violence*, Vol. 32, No. 5, 2018.

[15] Schuurman, 2018.

[16] Kamaldeep S. Bhui, Madelyn H. Hicks, Myrna Lashley, and Edgar Jones, "A Public Health Approach to Understanding and Preventing Violent Radicalization," *BMC Medicine*, Vol. 10, No. 1, 2012.

[17] Bhui et al., 2012; Linda L. Dahlberg and Etienne G. Krug, "Violence: A Global Public Health Problem," in Etienne G. Krug, Linda L. Dahlberg, James A. Mercy, Anthony B. Zwi, and Rafael Lozano, eds., *World Report on Violence and Health*, Geneva: World Health Organization, 2002; Lorne L. Dawson, *Sketch of a Social Ecol-*

Figure 1.1
The Socioecological Model for Violence Prevention

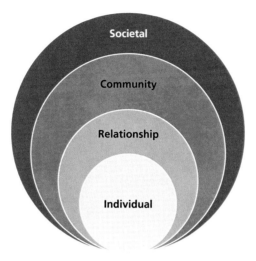

SOURCES: CDC, "The Social-Ecological Model: A Framework for Prevention," webpage, last reviewed January 28, 2021; the CDC developed the model from Dahlberg and Krug, 2002.

The model identifies four levels of factors that operate independently and in relationship with each other to affect both violent victimization and perpetration. At the core of the model are individuals' biological or historical factors that increase risk for victimization or perpetrating violence. Second, the model highlights the importance of relationships—specifically, family and peer groups. Third, the model asserts that characteristics of community institutions, such as schools, workplaces, health care, and criminal justice settings, can contribute to violence. Finally, there is the societal level, in which policies, social norms, and attitudes are the factors that can contribute to violence. In Chapter Two, we review research to date that has identified factors at each of these levels that increase vulnerability to radicalization.

Having an underlying model, such as this one, is helpful for at least two reasons. First, it provides an organizing framework for data surveillance: Data should be collected within each of these areas to identify modifiable factors at each level and relationships between levels that influence extremist violence. Second, a model provides guidance for prevention by acknowledging that efforts will likely be needed that expand across the levels of influence to create meaningful and sustained impact.

ogy Model for Explaining Homegrown Terrorist Radicalisation, The Hague, Netherlands: International Centre for Counter-Terrorism—The Hague, 2017.

Bhui and colleagues make another important point: A public health approach might also prioritize understanding the effect of radicalization and terrorist acts on social cohesion.[18] For example, accusations or suspicion that one is a terrorist or discrimination of a person or group thought to be terrorists could create social conditions (e.g., isolation, exclusion, unemployment) that may make some persons vulnerable to extremist ideology or violence. Family and friends of individuals who have radicalized may be an especially vulnerable group. Ensuring that families and friends of those who have radicalized are supported after learning that their family member or friend has radicalized may be a critical component for countering future radicalization and terrorist acts.

A Research Approach Derived from Suicide Prevention

To address the increasing call for more primary-source research in terrorism research,[19] as well as the call for considering public health approaches,[20] this project took an approach that has been used by public health researchers for decades to study suicide: the psychological autopsy. Psychological autopsies are postmortem, systematic interviews conducted by trained laypersons with family members and friends, often complemented by a record review, to learn about the person who died by suicide and the period before death.[21] This research strategy has resulted in findings that provide some of the strongest evidence to date that we have about suicide risk—specifically, that mental illness is common among the majority of those who die by suicide[22] and that members of households with firearms have a two- to tenfold increased risk of suicide compared with those in households without firearms.[23] Because of these results, suicide prevention strategies frequently involve increasing access to and quality of mental

---

[18] Bhui et al., 2012.

[19] Marc Sageman, "The Stagnation in Terrorism Research," *Terrorism and Political Violence*, Vol. 26, No. 4, 2014; Bart Schuurman and Quirine Eijkman, *Moving Terrorism Research Forward: The Crucial Role of Primary Sources*, The Hague, Netherlands: International Centre for Counter-Terrorism—The Hague, 2013.

[20] Bhui et al., 2012; National Academies of Sciences, Engineering, and Medicine, *Countering Violent Extremism Through Public Health Practice: Proceedings of a Workshop*, Washington, D.C.: National Academies Press, 2017.

[21] Kenneth R. Conner, Annette L. Beautrais, David A. Brent, Yeates Conwell, Michael R. Phillips, and Barbara Schneider, "The Next Generation of Psychological Autopsy Studies: Part I. Interview Content," *Suicide and Life-Threatening Behavior*, Vol. 41, No. 6, 2011.

[22] J. T. O. Cavanagh, A. J. Carson, M. Sharpe, and S. M. Lawrie, "Psychological Autopsy Studies of Suicide: A Systematic Review," *Psychological Medicine*, Vol. 33, No. 3, 2003.

[23] Deborah Azrael and Matthew J. Miller, "Reducing Suicide Without Affecting Underlying Mental Health," in Rory C. O'Connor and Jane Pirkis, eds., *The International Handbook of Suicide Prevention*, 2nd ed., Hoboken, N.J.: Wiley Blackwell, 2016.

health care and reducing access to firearms via policy or by encouraging safe storage practices.

Applying the psychological autopsy method to the study of radicalization and deradicalization is attractive because although suicide and extremism are distinct (though sometimes overlapping) phenomena, they share important attributes. First, they are both relatively rare events. Second, cases are rarely available to be interviewed because they are dead or, in the case of extremism, because interviewing those who have radicalized presents an assortment of ethical and logistical challenges, as many, if alive, are wary of providing incriminating evidence that can be used in legal proceedings. However, extremism is distinct because we are able to interview persons who have deradicalized; in fact, such individuals can provide compelling details about factors that were influential in that process. This is not directly comparable to interviewing persons who have survived a suicide attempt, but it is similar.

As described in Chapter Three, for the current study, we interviewed 12 family members of persons who have radicalized and 24 former extremists. We began by reviewing the limited past research drawing on interviews conducted with former extremists and their families.[24] At that point, in developing our interview protocol, we deviated somewhat from the psychological autopsy approach, which is semistructured and often includes specific questions to family about discrete constructs, such as mental health symptoms, in favor of an unstructured, narrative-based approach (described in more detail in Chapter Three). This shift was necessary because, unlike studies on suicide, research on extremism is less developed, and we did not identify specific hypotheses to test. Our less structured approach was designed to generate hypotheses rather than test them.

Limitations of the Approach

The psychological autopsy is not without its biases, many of which apply to the current study and should be considered before reading results. Family members who agree to be interviewed may be systematically different from those who refuse to participate. Similarly, individuals who have deradicalized and agree to be interviewed may be different from those who refuse to participate *and* from those who never deradicalize. Among those who are interviewed, respondents might not report truthfully or may recall things incorrectly (i.e., recall bias). For example, in RAND's own psychological autopsy study, family and friends were hard-pressed to answer questions about whether the decedent suffered from symptoms of posttraumatic stress disorder (PTSD) because they often could not provide valid information on whether or not the dece-

---

[24] See Chapter Two for an overview of the key findings from this literature.

dent had disturbing nightmares in the 30 days before death.[25] Also, our approach is a case series—we did not recruit nor interview a comparable control group. Therefore, we cannot state whether the factors or patterns we observed in our sample are more common than among a comparable group of individuals who did not join extremist organizations, which prohibits the calculation of risk or identification of risk factors.

There are other biases in our approach, some of which are common to studying victims or perpetrators of violent acts after the violence occurred. For example, many people exhibit mental health symptoms and are never formally diagnosed, and asking about mental health after a person has committed a violent act may be tautological. As described in a commentary on mass shootings: "'Why did this man do this terrible thing?' *Because he is mentally ill.* 'And how do you know he is mentally ill?' *Because he did this terrible thing.*"[26] In addition, as will be described in Chapter Three, our sample consists of 36 interviews (32 focal individuals); these individual cases are unlikely to be representative of all those who have radicalized (although we contend that it is challenging if not impossible to draw a representative sample of radicalized individuals). Finally, as shown in Chapter Three and in Appendix B, the interview protocol for this study was largely unstructured. This was done intentionally because there was very little precedent available to develop a structured protocol. Interviewers were trained to cover certain topical areas, but the interview was largely driven by the interviewee's experiences. Thus, our interviews did not systematically cover every potential question, and the absence of information on a particular topic, such as use of the internet during the radicalization process, does not signify that it did not exist.

Although these limitations and potential biases are important to keep in mind, they should not diminish the importance of the perspectives offered from participants during their interviews, particularly in a field where personal accounts are rare. Study results can be used to generate hypotheses for future research. When considered with existing literature, the results can confirm past findings or, conversely, call findings into question. The findings can also be used to identify policy and practice solutions that might still be helpful for preventing future radicalization in the United States. We distill what we identify as important themes across all of these areas in the concluding chapter of this report.

---

[25] Rajeev Ramchand, Enchanté Franklin, Elizabeth Thornton, Sarah Deland, and Jeffrey Rouse, "Opportunities to Intervene? 'Warning Signs' for Suicide in the Days Before Dying," *Death Studies*, Vol. 41, No. 6, 2017.

[26] J. Skeem and E. Mulvey, "What Role Does Serious Mental Illness Play in Mass Shootings, and How Should We Address It?" *Criminology and Public Policy*, Vol. 19, No. 1, 2020, p. 86.

Organization of This Report

The remainder of the report is structured as follows: In the next chapter (Chapter Two), we summarize the findings from the relevant body of literature to provide background for our interview analysis. In Chapter Three, we describe how we recruited individuals to be interviewed, our interview process, and our analysis of the qualitative data (appendixes at the end of the report provide a more detailed description of our methods). In Chapter Four, we describe characteristics of our sample across multiple levels of the socioecological framework. In Chapter Five, we describe themes in individuals' pathways to radicalization and activities individuals were involved in within extremist organizations. In Chapter Six, we describe how individuals deradicalized or left extremist organizations. Chapter Seven takes a citizen science perspective and offers recommendations from our interviewees about how radicalization could be mitigated and deradicalization encouraged. Finally, Chapter Eight synthesizes results across the previous chapters and offers recommendations for both research and practice.

CHAPTER TWO

Overview of the Literature

To inform our research and provide a framework for organizing the findings of our interviews, we conducted a targeted review of the body of academic literature concerning radicalization and deradicalization (or, more broadly, exit) of U.S. citizens or individuals who were radicalized while residing in the United States. Our literature review focused on studies that conducted primary- or original-data collection through interviews, surveys, or other targeted data collection with the radicalized or deradicalized individuals themselves or their family members or friends and were published in credible—ideally peer-reviewed—journals between the years 2000 and 2020. Given this study's focus on radicalization inside the United States, we chose to focus this review on domestic radicalization research, although we recognize that international radicalization research serves as a critical resource for understanding the radicalization and deradicaliza-

The PIRUS Database

The Profiles of Individual Radicalization in the United States (PIRUS) database is arguably the most influential and comprehensive database on the topic of domestic radicalization.[a] It is a database of "2,226 Islamist, far-left, far-right, and single-issue extremists who have radicalized to violent and non-violent extremism in the United States from 1948 through 2018."[b] Although the database does not solely contain information from primary sources, it does include information from interviews with radicalized or formerly radicalized individuals and their family, friends, or associates.

[a] National Consortium for the Study of Terrorism and Responses to Terrorism, University of Maryland, Profiles of Individual Radicalization in the United States, database, undated-a.

[b] National Consortium for the Study of Terrorism and Responses to Terrorism, University of Maryland, "Profiles of Individual Radicalization in the United States (PIRUS)," College Park, May 2020, p. 1.

tion process. Many research studies we reviewed were based on the PIRUS database. Further details on the methods and scope of this literature review can be found in Appendix A. The results of our review are summarized by topic in the subsequent sections.

Sources of Risk or Resiliency Associated with Radicalization

Risk Factors or Vulnerabilities

The literature suggests that there are several factors associated with radicalization; although these factors do not definitively indicate whether an individual will become radicalized, they represent potential risks or vulnerabilities common among individuals who do engage in extremist behavior. These factors are numerous and interrelated but can broadly be categorized into the individual, familial, and community, societal, and cultural levels. These vulnerabilities are summarized Table 2.1.

Table 2.1
Summary of Indicators of Radicalization

Level	Indicators
Individual characteristics or circumstances	• Emotional and psychological vulnerabilities: As one study explained, "Radicalization indicators are often the observable effects of underlying psychological and emotional processes. These processes are complex and are driven by feelings of lost significance and community victimization, as well as the intense need for psychological and emotional rewards."[a] • Identity issues: Individuals often pursue extremism to "fulfill a search for personal identity, or to overcome a sense of vulnerability or diminished self-worth[;] individuals derive personal meaning and value through group membership or identification with a cause greater than themselves."[b] • Social isolation or exclusion or perceived discrimination: This includes feelings of disenfranchisement or marginalization from society at the individual level. • Perceived discrimination: This includes feelings of being targeted or treated unfairly by others. • Personal trauma or crisis: Personal events, such as loss of a family member or poor living conditions, can push an individual toward extremism.[c] • Belief in the legitimacy of violent extremist causes: Individuals may believe extremist narratives that violence is justified; these narratives often use such issues as collateral damage incurred in drone strikes to paint the United States as an aggressor against which violence is justified. • Lack of awareness of violent radicalization and recruitment: Individuals may be uninformed or misinformed about terrorist groups or politics and thus more susceptible to recruitment or malign influence. • Substance misuse issues: Individuals with addiction issues may be more vulnerable to recruitment or more prone to engage in violence. • Cognitive impairment, deficit, or inflexibility: Some studies suggest that individuals with cognitive disabilities or other cognitive issues may be more vulnerable to manipulation or recruitment or be predisposed to engage in extremist behavior.[d] • Mental health issues: Mental health issues, such as depression, suicidal ideation, or personality disorders, may increase a person's vulnerability to extremist ideology or behavior.[e] • Low socioeconomic status, poverty, or lack of opportunities: A lack of social or economic mobility or lack of educational opportunities could push individuals to seek alternative means of achieving their desired livelihoods; the promise of material incentives can play a role in pushing individuals toward radicalization.

Table 2.1—Continued

Level	Indicators
Family influence	• Family discord: Being raised by a single parent, experiencing the divorce or separation of parents, or other household issues may contribute to individual distress and vulnerability to extremist narratives. • Lack of parental supervision or support: Youth without strong parental guidance and oversight could be more prone to encounter and engage with extremist content online, for instance, or to fill their parental void with other authoritative figures, such as community or religious leaders (who could in some cases prove to be harmful influences or recruiters for extremist networks).
Community, societal, and cultural influence	• Isolation from mainstream society: Some communities are very insular and cut off from the rest of society, which could create conditions ripe for recruitment. • Perceived discrimination or victimization: This sense of discrimination or victimization can play out at the community and the individual level. • Belief in legitimacy of violent extremist causes: Belief in extremist narratives that violence is justified can also manifest at the community level if accompanied by feelings of community victimization (such as in the Somali community in Minnesota).[f] • Mistrust of law enforcement: Communities that feel targeted by or otherwise mistrust law enforcement may contribute to an environment susceptible to extremist recruiters. • Living in underserved, impoverished, or unsafe communities: Communities composed of immigrants, refugees, or other marginalized populations or communities with high crime rates may be more vulnerable to extremist narratives. • Contact with recruiters or radicalized individuals: Contact with recruiters or radicalized individuals, especially those in trusted familial or social circles with a great deal of influence over individuals, can directly result in radicalization.

[a] Michael Jensen, Gary LaFree, Patrick A. James, Anita Atwell-Seate, Daniela Pisoiu, John Stevenson, and Herbert Tinsley, *Empirical Assessment of Domestic Radicalization (EADR)*, College Park: National Consortium for the Study of Terrorism and Responses to Terrorism, University of Maryland, 2016.

[b] Jensen et al., 2016.

[c] Stevan Weine and Osman Ahmed, *Building Resilience to Violent Extremism Among Somali-Americans in Minneapolis-St. Paul*, College Park: National Consortium for the Study of Terrorism and Responses to Terrorism, University of Maryland, August 2012.

[d] Leor Zmigrod, Peter Jason Rentfrow, and Trevor W. Robbins, "Cognitive Inflexibility Predicts Extremist Attitudes," *Frontiers in Psychology*, Vol. 10, May 2019.

[e] Paul Gill, Caitlin Clemmow, Florian Hetzel, Bettina Rottweiler, Nadine Salman, Isabelle van der Vegt, Zoe Marchment, Sandy Schumann, Sanaz Zolghadriha, Norah Schulten, Helen Taylor, and Emily Corner, "Systematic Review of Mental Health Problems and Violent Extremism," *Journal of Forensic Psychiatry and Psychology*, Vol. 32, No. 1, 2021.

[f] Weine and Ahmed, 2012, p. 9: "We interviewed 57 persons who lived or worked in Minneapolis-St. Paul and who were either: 1) Somali-American young adult males (ages 16 to 30) (n=18); 2) Somali-American parents or adult family members (n=19); or 3) service providers who work with the Somali community (n=20). In this report, the term 'Somali-American' is not being used only to refer to U.S. citizens."

One important note regarding the vulnerabilities presented in Table 2.1 is that there is a lack of consensus surrounding the role of mental health in radicalization. Although there is a tendency among members of the general public and some in academia to chalk extremist behavior up to mental health issues, it is difficult to establish causation between mental health issues and extremist behavior, particularly because mental health symptoms (and perhaps many other individual attributes) are often not collected until after a person has joined a radical group. Thus, there may be bias in these methods. PIRUS data indicate that "extremists and terrorists are no more likely to suffer from mental health problems than members of the general population,"[1] with mental illness accounting for or coinciding with only a small percentage (a mean of ~11 percent) of the examined radicalization cases. However, in one study of former white supremacists, 32 percent of the sample reported experiencing mental health problems (that were unspecified in the report) before or during involvement in an extremist group, whereas 44 percent reported experiencing suicidal ideation.[2] By comparison, according to the National Institute of Mental Health, about 16 percent of the population in the United States as of 2019 suffers from some form of mental illness.[3] According to these findings, it appears that mental illness—if it predates entrance into an extremist organization—could potentially increase vulnerability to radicalization but is not a major driver on its own.[4]

Another vulnerability that contradicts conventional wisdom is the role of poverty or material incentives in domestic radicalization. The PIRUS data suggest that low socioeconomic status does not seem to be a major driver of radicalization in the United States, with only about 25 percent of radicalized individuals in the PIRUS sample coming from an impoverished background. Indeed, PIRUS data illustrate that "radicalization to violence is primarily psychological and emotional, rather than material."[5] Although material factors are rarely the main drivers of radicalization in the United States, some studies suggest that they can still contribute to radicalization when combined with other factors, described above.[6] Researchers behind the PIRUS effort

---

[1]   Jensen et al., 2016.

[2]   Bubolz and Simi, 2015.

[3]   National Institute of Mental Health, "Mental Illness," webpage, last updated January 2021.

[4]   One systematic review of mental health problems and violent extremism assessed that prevalence rates of mental health problems in individual studies ranged from 0 to 57 percent. Studies that drew on privileged access to police or judicial data suggested a rate of mental health problems of 16.96 percent. See Gill et al., 2021. A preliminary study of 76 extremists associated with Islamic State attacks against the West found a rate of a history of mental health problems of 27.6 percent. See Emily Corner and Paul Gill, "Is There a Nexus Between Terrorist Involvement and Mental Health in the Age of the Islamic State?" *CTC Sentinel*, Vol. 10, No. 1, 2017.

[5]   Jensen et al., 2016.

[6]   See, for example, Weine and Ahmed, 2012; Pete Simi, Steven Windisch, and Karyn Sporer, *Recruitment and Radicalization Among US Far-Right Terrorists*, College Park: National Consortium for the Study of Terrorism and Responses to Terrorism, University of Maryland, November 2016.

noted that lack of educational opportunity also did not play a major role in most of the examined cases, observing: "The conventional wisdom that radicalization is more common among individuals who come from low [socioeconomic status] backgrounds and/or lack educational opportunities is generally not supported by the PIRUS data. Most extremists come from middle class backgrounds and have at least some college education."[7]

Although there is no single radicalization process, one prominent analysis of PIRUS data found that the most powerful combination of risk factors may be "pathways that combine individual psychological and emotional vulnerabilities with perceptions of community victimization."[8] According to this study, psychological and emotional vulnerabilities are feelings that "stem from lost significance, personal trauma, and collective crises."[9] *Community victimization* refers to the perception that an individual's community is being unfairly targeted or marginalized;[10] a study of risk factors in the Somali American community in Minneapolis–Saint Paul, for instance, found that issues with U.S. foreign policy toward and media coverage of Somalia engendered feelings of resentment and marginalization among some in the community and contributed to the perceived social legitimacy of violent extremism.[11] Another notable theory in the literature suggests that the "quest for significance" can drive individuals to engage in extremism. As the authors of another PIRUS-based study explained,

---

[7]   Jensen et al., 2016. International research on the topic of poverty is also insightful. Krueger and Malečková famously documented no relationship between poverty and education and Palestinian support for attacks against Israel (Alan B. Krueger and Jitka Malečková, "Education, Poverty and Terrorism: Is There a Causal Connection?" *Journal of Economic Perspectives*, Vol. 17, No. 4, 2003). More recently, Dawson and Amarasingam found in their conversations with Western recruits for ISIS that socioeconomic factors played little role in their radicalization (Lorne L. Dawson and Amarnath Amarasingam, "Talking to Foreign Fighters: Insights into the Motivations for Hijrah to Syria and Iraq," *Studies in Conflict and Terrorism*, Vol. 40, No. 3, 2017). An ethnographic study of Dutch foreign fighters, though, suggested that such factors were important (Daan Weggemanns, Edwin Bakker, and Peter Grol, "Who Are They and Why Do They Go? The Radicalisation and Preparatory Processes of Dutch Jihadist Foreign Fighters," *Perspectives on Terrorism*, Vol. 8, No. 4, 2014). A recently published systematic scoping review of the radicalization literature identified unemployment as an important push factor for extremism (Matteo Vergani, Muhammad Iqbal, Ekin Ilbahar, and Greg Barton, "The Three Ps of Radicalization: Push, Pull and Personal; A Systematic Scoping Review of the Scientific Evidence About Radicalization into Violent Extremism," *Studies in Conflict and Terrorism*, Vol. 43, No. 10, 2020). Finally, a meta-analysis of risk factors for radicalization found that unemployment ranked only as one of the "smallest" effects on risk (Michael Wolfowicz, Yael Litmanovitz, David Weisburd, and Badi Hasisi, "A Field-Wide Systematic Review and Meta-Analysis of Putative Risk and Protective Factors for Radicalization Outcomes," *Journal of Quantitative Criminology*, Vol. 36, 2020).

[8]   Jensen et al., 2016. A systematic scoping review noted that perceived injustice was an important push factor into extremism (Vergani et al., 2020). A common refrain those authors noted relates to jihadist fears of Western policies targeting Muslims in Afghanistan and elsewhere. Also see Todd C. Helmus, "Why and How Some People Become Terrorists," in Paul K. Davis and Kim Cragin, eds., *Social Science for Counterterrorism: Putting the Pieces Together*, Santa Monica, Calif.: RAND Corporation, MG-849-OSD, 2008.

[9]   Jensen et al., 2016, p. 6.

[10]   Jensen et al., 2016.

[11]   Weine and Ahmed, 2012.

When people perceive themselves as rejected, divested of control, or as victims of injustice, they feel belittled and disrespected; consequently, they are motivated to restore their sense of self-worth and meaning. According to the significance quest theory . . . the need for personal significance makes the occurrence of extreme behavior more likely. Propelled by such needs, people should be more likely to fully commit to important goals and to suppress other concerns because the former are especially well-suited to restoring their sense of meaning and personal significance.[12]

The research team involved in that study conducted logistic regression analysis to determine which specific aspects of loss of significance, if any, were correlated with violent behavior and found that "most of the indicators of loss of significance were positively related to the probability of political violence. At the bivariate level when individuals experienced failure at work, when they were rejected in social relationships, or when they were victims of abuse, they were more likely to resort to violence to pursue their ideological goals."[13]

Sources of Resilience to Radicalization

In addition to the risk factors described above, there are some factors that are likely to *decrease* an individual's vulnerability to radicalization and risk of engaging in violent extremism. These factors—often referred to as *protective factors*—overlap heavily with sources of resiliency against engaging in crime.[14] Hypothesized protective factors include stable employment history, age, marital status, and strength of the family unit.[15] Stable employment can decrease an individual's risk of adopting extremist beliefs and, once someone is radicalized, can also decrease the risk that the individual actually acts on these beliefs and engages in extremist behavior. As one study explained: "[S]table employment may decrease the risk that individuals with extreme views will engage in violent behaviors. Stable employment often leads to the development of positive social relationships and places demands on individuals' time that depress extremist activities."[16] In comparing a sample from PIRUS with a control group, one study found that, as with nonextremist criminal behavior, individuals are less likely to engage in violent extremism the older they become.[17] This is not always the case, however; white

[12] Katarzyna Jasko, Gary LaFree, and Arie Kruglanski, "Quest for Significance and Violent Extremism: The Case of Domestic Radicalization," *Political Psychology*, Vol. 38, No. 5, 2017, p. 818.

[13] Jasko, LaFree, and Kruglanski, 2020, p. 828.

[14] Simi, Windisch, and Sporer, 2016.

[15] Bubolz and Simi, 2015.

[16] Jensen et al., 2016.

[17] Jensen et al., 2016.

supremacists tended to radicalize later in life,[18] as do members of single-issue groups. Finally, married individuals and those who have strong family units (including youth with strong parental supervision and support) tend to be less susceptible to radicalization and recruitment.[19]

Demographic Characteristics and Other Attributes of Radicalized Populations

The literature illustrates that the three major extremist ideologies currently present in the United States are *far right, far left*, and *Islamist*. The PIRUS database, in particular, provides a robust picture of the ideological leanings and demographic profiles of radicalized individuals. Of the 2,226 people examined in the PIRUS database, the overwhelming majority fell into these three ideological groups, with 977 individuals adhering to far-right extremism, 511 adhering to Islamic extremism, and 374 adhering to far-left extremism. We compared the three groups demographically and found quite a bit of variation across categories, although some common themes emerge. Table 2.2 summarizes the salient attributes across the three examined extremist ideologies.

As the data show, the most consistent thread across all groups is the percentage of radicalized individuals in each group who come from a low socioeconomic status (~22 percent mean). On average, far-right extremists are in their late 30s at the time of (known) radicalization, they are overwhelmingly male, about three-fourths do not have a college education, and about a quarter have a violent criminal background. A greater percentage of far-right extremists have a military background (29.2 percent) than individuals in the other groups. Within far-right extremism, the main tenet is white supremacy (65 percent), followed by antigovernment sentiment (28.9 percent) and anti-immigrant sentiment (10.3 percent).[20] In comparison, both far-left and Islamic extremists are around 29, on average, at the time of radicalization and have similar rates of prior military experience (~11 percent) and violent criminal history (~11 percent). Far-left extremist groups have far more females (24.4 percent) than the other groups and have attained higher levels of education. Within far-left extremism, the main subideology is animal rights and environmentalism, followed by new leftism and black nationalism, anticapitalism, and anarchism.[21] Although mental illness did not appear to be a major factor across any of the ideologies, Islamists have the

---

[18] Michael Jensen, Patrick James, and Elizabeth Yates, "Contextualizing Disengagement: How Exit Barriers Shape the Pathways Out of Far-Right Extremism in the United States," *Studies in Conflict and Terrorism*, May 4, 2020.

[19] Stevan Weine, Schuyler Henderson, Stephen Shanfield, Rupinder Legha, and Jerrold Post, "Building Community Resilience to Counter Violent Extremism," *Democracy and Security*, Vol. 9, No. 4, 2013; Weine and Ahmed, 2012, p. 2.

[20] Michael Jensen, Patrick James, Gary LaFree, and Aaron Safer-Lichtenstein, "Pre-Radicalization Criminal Activity of United States Extremists," College Park: National Consortium for the Study of Terrorism and Responses to Terrorism, University of Maryland, January 2018.

[21] Jensen, James, LaFree, and Safer-Lichtenstein, 2018.

Table 2.2
Extremist Attributes Across Ideologies

Ideology	Age at Time of Known Radicalization (mean years)	Gender (% female)	Education Level (% with college degree or higher)	Socioeconomic Status (% coming from low socioeconomic stratum)	Immigrant Status (% immigrants)	U.S. Military Background (% with prior or current U.S. military service)	Child Abuse (% with history of abuse as a minor)	Mental Health Issues (% with professional diagnoses)	Substance Misuse (% with evidence of alcohol/drug misuse)	History of Violent Criminal Activity (% with this background)
Islamist	30.08	4.1	41.1	20.4	60.7	10.5	4.1	4.1	7.6	11.1
Far right	37.76	4.7	25.4	25.3	1.3	29.2	2.7	1.8	10.1	25.7
Far left	28.21	24.4	55.2	19.7	5.0	11.3	3.3	2.0	5.6	11.9

SOURCE: Compiled from PIRUS data as presented in Jensen et al., 2016.

highest rates of mental illness among the three groups. Across the variables examined in PIRUS, far leftists and Islamists share more common characteristics—apart from immigrant status and percentage of females—than do the far left and far right or the far-right and Islamist groups.

Pathways to Radicalization

The literature suggests that there is no single model of or pathway to radicalization. As one study based on the PIRUS database assessed, "Significant background, demographic and radicalization differences are present across the ideological spectrum, and the processes by which individuals and groups come to engage in extremist behaviors are complex, often resulting from a host of psychological and emotional factors that are difficult to model."[22] In short, individuals usually do not radicalize for a singular reason; instead, there are multiple factors—many of them covered under our previous discussion of risk factors—that converge to spark radicalization. There are, however, some common vehicles or mediums through which radicalization processes tend to occur.

Some studies, for instance, posit that online radicalization is becoming the most prevalent pathway to radicalization, with the internet serving as the most common vehicle for radicalization across ideological groups.[23] The internet is not only increasing the reach of radicalization but also appears to be shortening the timeline for radicalization. Traditionally, the radicalization process may take years, but "recent evidence . . . suggests that online environments may be speeding up radicalization processes, reducing them to several months in many cases."[24] Another common pathway to radicalization appears to be engaging in criminal activity. A substantial percentage of radicalized individuals in the PIRUS data and in the groups of former radicalized individuals interviewed in other studies engaged in crime prior to radicalization (in PIRUS, a mean of 39 percent across groups). This suggests that crime can serve as a gateway to radicalization—or at least indicate a proclivity for violent behavior.

In other countries, prisons have served as major vehicles for radicalization; this appears to be less so in the United States thus far. According to PIRUS data, "The rates of prison radicalization in the U.S. are low and even across the ideological spectrum,

---

[22] Jensen et al., 2016.

[23] Michael Jensen, Patrick James, Gary LaFree, Aaron Safer-Lichtenstein, and Elizabeth Yates, *The Use of Social Media by United States Extremists*, College Park: National Consortium for the Study of Terrorism and Responses to Terrorism, University of Maryland, 2018.

[24] National Institute of Justice, "Research Provides Guidance on Building Effective Counterterrorism Programs," July 8, 2018.

suggesting that it is not a common pathway for most extremists nor is it limited to a particular ideology."[25]

Additionally, several studies argue that radicalization in the United States generally occurs in waves that correspond with the rise of different ideologies (i.e., Islamist, far-right, and far-left ideologies). The attacks of 9/11, for instance, were a clear trigger for Islamic extremism becoming more widespread in the United States. This suggests a sort of group-think-driven momentum behind the prevalence and propagation of ideologies.

For a more in-depth analysis of radicalization pathways, Simi and colleagues' study of former white supremacists provides a helpful analysis.[26] In analyzing pull factors, they noted that former white supremacists routinely highlighted the support and camaraderie received as members of the movement. Other factors, which helped serve as driving motivations, included the "thrill of the forbidden" or a desire for thrill seeking, a desire for protection, and a quest for significance. The authors also identified pathways for enlistment into extremism and offer a description of the various approaches by which participants were recruited into extremism. They also highlight the unique role that white power music represents as a critical conduit into extremism.

Finally, although "lone wolf" actors have garnered increasing attention in domestic counterterrorism efforts, studies found that radicalization remains a social process, meaning that radicalized individuals usually join extremist groups rather than acting alone. For lone wolves, the primary vectors for radicalization were (in ranked order): the internet, nonmilitary workplaces, the military, membership in or interaction with extremist groups, prison or jail, and adverse government experiences.[27]

Processes of Exiting Extremist Organizations

Another set of questions we explored through the literature review concerned processes of exiting extremism. Our review sought to answer the following questions: What are the processes through which individuals become deradicalized or otherwise disengaged from radical behavior? What are the primary factors that contribute to deradicalization?

Defining *Exit* from Extremism

Broadly speaking, *exit* from groups can take many forms that entail various levels of removal or disassociation from extremist ideology and behavior. The following terms are frequently used in the literature to describe these phases or forms of exit:

---

[25] Jensen et al., 2016.

[26] Simi, Windisch, and Sporer, 2016.

[27] Mark Hamm and Ramon Spaaij, "Lone Wolf Terrorism in America: Using Knowledge of Radicalization Pathways to Forge Prevention Strategies," Indiana State University, 2015.

- *Disengagement* is defined in the literature as "disassociating with extremist groups or individuals by ending behaviors related to extremism"[28] or "the process of withdrawing from the normative expectations associated with a role, the process whereby an individual no longer accepts as appropriate the socially defined rights and obligations that accompany a given role in society."[29] Disengagement does not necessarily mean abandonment of extremist beliefs, however, with one study noting: "Disengagement is not really the end of that [extremist] identity. Instead, a whole other layer of unwanted and involuntary thoughts, feelings, bodily reactions, and behaviors may persist and continue to shape a person's life."[30]
- *Deradicalization*, as previously defined, is "the process of changing an individual's belief system, rejecting the extremist ideology, and embracing mainstream values."[31] Deradicalization is a step beyond disengagement, as it signals a "more complete cognitive shift or transformation" away from extremism;[32] in other words, true deradicalization entails abandoning or renouncing extremist beliefs rather than just ceasing extremist behavior.
- *Defection* entails "'physically separating from the group and resolving not to go back,' but does not necessarily mean that an individual has [forgone] group beliefs."[33]
- *Desistance* typically indicates "changes in severity or frequency of criminal offending."[34]

The main types of exit covered in the literature include the following:

- *Expulsion* occurs when individuals are forced to leave the group by leaders or other members.
- *Extraction* occurs when an outsider forces or enables the individual to leave.
- *Voluntary exit* occurs when an individual leaves of his or her own volition.

One study that involved interviewing former white supremacists identified five phases of exit:

---

[28] Pete Simi, Kathleen Blee, Matthew DeMichele, and Steven Windisch, "Addicted to Hate: Identity Residual Among Former White Supremacists," *American Sociological Review*, Vol. 82, No. 6, 2017.

[29] Bubolz and Simi, 2015, p. 5.

[30] Simi et al., 2017.

[31] Bubolz and Simi, 2015.

[32] Simi et al., 2017.

[33] Bubolz and Simi, 2015, quoting R. W. Balch, "When the Light Goes Out, Darkness Comes: A Study of Defection from a Totalistic Cult," in R. Stark, ed., *Religious Movements: Genesis, Exodus, and Numbers*, New York: Paragon House, 1986.

[34] Bubolz and Simi, 2015.

1. *Motivation* is when "an individual is still part of the movement, but is beginning to doubt involvement."[35]
2. *Disengagement* is when "the person has made the decision to leave the movement."[36]
3. *Establishment* is when "the individual has left the movement and has a place to live."[37]
4. *Reflection* is when "individuals begin to realize the extent of their extremist ideology, violence, and criminal actions while involved in the movement."[38]
5. *Stabilization* is when "individuals have a normal life and perhaps a family."[39]

Main Factors Leading to Exit

As with radicalization, there is no standard model of exit from extremist groups, with one study of former white supremacists finding that "no single reason for leaving cuts across the majority of the sample."[40] The literature did suggest that there is a great deal of overlap between exiting gangs, cults, and extremist organizations. Although there is a lot of variation in motives for leaving, several common motives do emerge in the literature. Similar to the process of radicalization, there are also *push* and *pull factors* that contribute to an individual's exit from extremism. Push factors are those "negative considerations that induce members to leave," while pull factors are "positive considerations that attract members to another life."[41] Figure 2.1 summarizes these factors.

Postexit Issues

The literature suggests that exit from extremist organizations is rarely complete or final. Several respondents across studies of former extremists reported ideological relapse; in one study, 21 percent of former white supremacists reported leaving their respective extremist organization and later returning to the group.[42] In this sense, there are similarities between radicalization and addiction, with former extremists tending to feel a lingering "addiction" to the cause. One study termed this "habitual and unwanted thoughts, feelings, physiological responses, and behavior that can follow exit" as "residual" or "hangover" identity.[43] In some cases, the study noted, "You are withdrawing

---

[35] Bubolz and Simi, 2015.

[36] Bubolz and Simi, 2015.

[37] Bubolz and Simi, 2015.

[38] Bubolz and Simi, 2015.

[39] Bubolz and Simi, 2015.

[40] Bubolz and Simi, 2015.

[41] Bubolz and Simi, 2015.

[42] Bubolz and Simi, 2015.

[43] Simi et al., 2017.

Figure 2.1
Summary of Push and Pull Factors for Exit from Extremist Groups

Push factors	Pull factors

• Disillusionment
• Inability to maintain employment
• Experiencing negative effects of violence
• **Burnout or exhaustion:** According to one study, "some individuals may begin to burn out because of the demanding lifestyle and guilt produced from engaging in violence." This phenomenon is particularly prevalent among members of white supremacist organizations, with "previous studies not[ing] the high burn-out rate among members of the white supremacist movement and the substantial retention efforts initiated by various groups to sustain participation."[a]
• **Physical factors,** such as experience of imprisonment or incarceration (although, as previously noted, this could also contribute to further radicalization)
• **Dissatisfaction with a group's activities,** including differences in expectation versus reality or moral qualms
• **Distrust of or lack of loyalty among group leadership or other members:** One study found variation between ideological groups for this factor, noting: "While left-wing participants often indicated that distrust stemmed from a lack of support from group members following victimization from external entities, right-wing participants discussed internal violence between members as contributing to perceptions of distrust."[b]
• **Perceptions of low ability, low integrity, and low benevolence of group**[c]
	• **Diminished "biographical availability,"**[d] including
	  – marital responsibilities and raising children
	  – positive role of significant others
	  – maturing out of the movement and desiring a more conventional lifestyle
	• **Groupthink or sense of security** in numbers can prompt exit of multiple people at same time; the literature reflects trends of leaving as small groups:
	  – sometimes individuals leave the group with romantic partners or smaller groups of people
	  – 21% of people in one study left the movement at same time as other members
	  – 35% of participants who were married left with their spouse (who was also involved in group)

[a] Simi et al., 2017.
[b] Steven Windisch, Gina Scott Ligon, and Pete Simi, "Organizational [Dis]trust: Comparing Disengagement Among Former Left-Wing and Right-Wing Violent Extremists," *Studies in Conflict and Terrorism,* Vol. 42, No. 6, 2019.
[c] Windisch, Ligon, and Simi, 2019.
[d] Bubolz and Simi, 2015.

from an old psychological status and coming into a new, and in doing so something akin to the withdrawal symptoms of drug addiction occurs."[44] The similarities between exit from extremism and postaddiction issues have implications for designing interventions, as "effective interventions may require much greater attention to the enduring qualities of extremism in order to offset residual-related issues."[45]

---

[44] Simi et al., 2017.

[45] Simi et al., 2017.

Perspectives on Mitigation Strategies for Extremism

Our initial literature review revealed few insights about how "formers" or family members, friends, and others touched by radicalization felt that the experience they went through could have been prevented or minimized, a topic we cover in Chapter Seven. However, there is a limited evaluation literature describing what is effective at mitigating violent extremism and what types of approaches are currently being used.

At the time of writing, there were only a limited number of studies—many of them conducted by RAND—that rigorously examined the impact of CVE programming. All of the studies reported positive outcomes: Process evaluations indicated that programs were successfully implemented,[46] and some interventions changed attitudes.[47] However, these studies generally employed weak evaluation designs, limiting any conclusions we can make about the program effects or our ability to compare different approaches. This is especially true of programs in the West, since only four studies were conducted with U.S. or European populations.

RAND evaluated domestic CVE programming in the United States published in a 2019 report titled *Practical Terrorism Prevention: Reexamining U.S. National Approaches to Addressing the Threat of Ideologically Motivated Violence*.[48] Using a review of national-level terrorism programming and local-level programming in five states (California, Texas, Colorado, Massachusetts, and Minnesota), the study identified a variety of gaps in existing programming and produced numerous findings pertaining to what contributes to effective CVE programming. The high-level findings most relevant to our study are (1) "community education efforts, formation of public-private partnerships, and development of local capacity to intervene with individuals at risk of radicalizing to violence" have been areas of success in U.S. CVE programming; (2) programs in which the federal government plays a supporting rather than leading role—by supporting "state, local, nongovernmental, and private organizations' terrorism prevention efforts through funding and other mechanisms"—are most effective; and (3) programs implemented by multidisciplinary teams that include members of

---

[46] D. P. Aldrich, "First Steps Towards Hearts and Minds? USAID's Countering Violent Extremism Policies in Africa," *Terrorism and Political Violence*, Vol. 26, No. 3, 2014; Ross Frenett and Moli Dow, *One to One Online Interventions: A Pilot CVE Methodology*, London: Institute for Strategic Dialogue and Curtain University, 2014.

[47] Allard Rienk Feddes, Liesbeth Mann, and Bertjan Doosje, "Increasing Self-Esteem and Empathy to Prevent Violent Radicalization: A Longitudinal Quantitative Evaluation of a Resilience Training Focused on Adolescents with a Dual Identity," *Journal of Applied Social Psychology*, Vol. 45, No. 7, 2015; Michael J. Williams, John G. Horgan, and William P. Evans, "The Critical Role of Friends in Networks for Countering Violent Extremism: Toward a Theory of Vicarious Help-Seeking," *Behavioral Sciences of Terrorism and Political Aggression*, Vol. 8, No. 1, 2016; Frenett and Dow, 2014.

[48] Brian A. Jackson, Ashley L. Rhoades, Jordan R. Reimer, Natasha Lander, Katherine Costello, and Sina Beaghley, *Practical Terrorism Prevention: Reexamining U.S. National Approaches to Addressing the Threat of Ideologically Motivated Violence*, Homeland Security Operational Analysis Center operated by the RAND Corporation, RR-2647-DHS, 2019b.

the local community tend to be successful.[49] The authors did not interview or examine firsthand accounts of how radicalized individuals responded to such interventions, however.

In 2020, RAND published another evaluation of CVE programming—a "tech camp" training and a "peace promotion fellowship"—in the Philippines.[50] To complement this evaluation, RAND also conducted a review of existing literature on CVE programming in the Philippines to provide future implementers with potential best practices.[51] Although these two reports are highly specific to the Philippines and are thus difficult to generalize to other countries or contexts, they do suggest that, similar to one of the conclusions from the *Practical Terrorism Prevention* report, micro-CVE campaigns—meaning those run by members of the local community and targeting others in the community for outreach or intervention—may be better positioned than the government to counter extremism.

RAND has also conducted nonevaluative environmental scans to identify the types of CVE programs operating in the United States and abroad. In a 2017 review, RAND interviewed representatives from 30 programs both in the United States and abroad that were focused on preventing Islamic and other forms of extremism.[52] Although not representative of all programs working to counter violent extremism, many were established by formers, family members, and friends and work with *individuals* who are at risk of radicalization (e.g., helping youth develop the skills to effectively distinguish true Islamic principles from extremist ideology) or *parents or community members* who could in turn influence individuals who were at risk (e.g., engaging parents to help them understand terrorist threats and what they should do if they see a threat).

An overview of the findings from this work provides insights into what organizations believe are influential causes of radicalization and terrorism, as well as their thoughts about how radicalization and terrorism can be prevented. For example, programs predicated on the idea that radicalization is caused in large part by the persuasive power of recruiting organizations seek to foster prosocial ideological beliefs among individuals at risk. Other organizations may operate under the theory that affiliating

---

[49] Brian A. Jackson, Ashley L. Rhoades, Jordan R. Reimer, Natasha Lander, Katherine Costello, and Sina Beaghley, "Building an Effective and Practical National Approach to Terrorism Prevention," Homeland Security Operational Analysis Center operated by the RAND Corporation, RB-10030-DHS, 2019a.

[50] See Ashley L. Rhoades, Todd C. Helmus, James V. Marrone, Victoria M. Smith, and Elizabeth Bodine-Baron, *Promoting Peace as the Antidote to Violent Extremism: Evaluation of a Philippines-Based Tech Camp and Peace Promotion Fellowship*, Santa Monica, Calif.: RAND Corporation, RR-A233-3, 2020.

[51] See Ashley L. Rhoades and Todd C. Helmus, *Countering Violent Extremism in the Philippines: A Snapshot of Current Challenges and Responses*, Santa Monica, Calif.: RAND Corporation, RR-A233-2, 2020.

[52] Sina Beaghley, Todd C. Helmus, Miriam Matthews, Rajeev Ramchand, David Stebbins, Amanda Kadlec, and Michael A. Brown, *Development and Pilot Test of the RAND Program Evaluation Toolkit for Countering Violent Extremism*, Santa Monica, Calif.: RAND Corporation, RR-1799-DHS, 2017.

with deviant peers is a root cause of radicalization and thus seek to enhance positive social networks. Some organizations work to improve social or economic integration or create environments accepting of minority groups, believing that systemic forces, such as marginalization and discrimination, influence radicalization. Figure 2.2 provides a list of objectives representative of the 30 programs RAND interviewed.

Conclusion

There is a limited, though growing, literature on extremism based on personal accounts of current and former extremists, as well as their family and friends. Existing work highlights individual, familial, and community, social, and cultural factors that have been hypothesized to be associated with radicalization. However, caution should be raised when attributing any of these factors with radicalization, as many of the factors are common in the population (and therefore not deterministic) and may influence different parts of a person's journey into extremism or may be indirectly associated with extremism. The literature also indicates heterogeneity in pathways to radicalization and, for those who leave extremist groups, heterogeneity in deradicalization. There are groups actively working to prevent violent extremism in the United States using a variety of approaches and an expanding literature evaluating these approaches.

Figure 2.2
Objectives for CVE Community-Based Programs

 Programs targeting individuals at risk

- Counter violent extremist and racist opinions and ideology
- Improve psychological conditions and address moral concerns
- Enhance positive social networks
- Reduce political grievances
- Improve social and economic integration

 Programs targeting community members

- Help community members understand and identify violent extremism and risks
- Build the capacity of community members to identify and engage with at-risk individuals
- Build the capacity of positive and influential members or leaders of the community to credibly counter violent extremist ideology
- Create environments accepting of minority groups
- Promote policies that address political grievances
- Strengthen government capacity to curtail violent extremism

SOURCE: Beagley et al., 2017.

CHAPTER THREE

Methods

Project Design

Our primary-data collection method involved semistructured interviews with former members of radical extremist organizations, as well as their family members, followed by team-based structured qualitative analysis of these interview transcripts. In this chapter, we describe our interview methods.

Using a convenience-sampling approach, RAND partnered with two nonprofit organizations to recruit interview participants—Parents for Peace and Beyond Barriers. Both of these organizations work with former members of radical extremist groups (referred to as *formers* or *focal individuals*), as well as family members who have assisted with deradicalization efforts.

Parents for Peace and Beyond Barriers reached out to their members using an email script approved by RAND's Institutional Review Board (Human Subjects Protection Committee [HSPC]) to gauge their interest in being interviewed. If potential participants indicated interest, our partners posted an email contact for each potential participant on a secure spreadsheet accessible to both RAND and our partners. Using a different HSPC-approved email script, RAND attempted to schedule interviews with 49 of the 57 contacts received. Recruitment efforts with two refusals for participation and one no-show resulted in a 73 percent response rate, in which 36 interviews were completed (see Chapter Four for a detailed description of the sample).

Sample Demographics and Case Details

Among the 32 cases, 24 interviews were conducted with the person him or herself, and 12 were conducted only with a family member or friend. For four cases, two interviews were conducted per case, including the focal individual and a family member (three cases) or two family members or friends (one case). Our 36 respondents provided background information on 32 focal individuals' upbringing, length of involvement in extreme organizations, and other related factors. We present this information in Table 3.1.

Parents for Peace and Beyond Barriers

Parents for Peace is a nonprofit that develops family and peer-centered solutions to the challenge of extremism. Founded in 2015 by family members of the man who committed the fatal 2009 Little Rock shooting, Parents for Peace has established a growing alliance of people affected by extremism, including family members of individuals who radicalized, survivors of extremist violence, and former extremists. Parents for Peace fosters a supportive environment while amplifying these credible voices via social media and public speaking to improve understanding of this complex issue. Parents for Peace established an independent helpline for people with concerns about a loved one becoming involved in extremism. Parents for Peace is also working to inspire the next generation to take on this topic by connecting with Boston University classes involved in the "P2P: Challenging Extremism" competition.

Beyond Barriers is a nonprofit dedicated to helping radicalized individuals leave extremist organizations. Founded by a former leader of the NSM, the largest neo-Nazi organization in the United States, the disengagement and deradicalization approach of Beyond Barriers centers on providing support and connecting individuals and communities affected by extremism to resources. In addition, Beyond Barriers is committed to educating communities and policymakers on how to optimize the reintegration of former radicals into society. To support its mission, it maintains a widely available podcast, an up-to-date commentary page on its website, and a social media presence.

Nine of the 32 focal individuals were women. Of the 18 focal individuals who described the type of area in which they grew up, seven described it as rural and 13 as urban or suburban. Two-thirds of focal individuals were white supremacists.

We also summarized information in interviews that helps describe the nature of our 32 cases. Over half of the cases discussed were involved in radical activities starting in the 2000s, while six were involved in radical activities before the 2000s, and in six more cases, they were involved in both eras. We determined that just over half of our 32 focal individuals had a *violent intent*, which we identified by any mention in the interviews of involvement in violent activities or planned violent activities during their time in extreme organizations.

Respondents described being involved with several organizations they considered extreme, including those listed in Table 3.2. We determined that 15 of the cases described being involved in two or more radical organizations over the course of their lives. The majority of cases centered on three of the organizations listed in Table 3.2.

Table 3.1
Summary of Individuals Involved in Radicalization

Characteristic	Number
Total cases	32
Type of radical involvement	
White supremacist	24
Islamic extremist	8
Gender	
Female	9
Male	23
Childhood setting	
Rural	7
Urban or suburban	13
Unclear	12
Era involved in radicalization	
Pre-2000s	6
2000s	17
Both eras	6
Unknown	3
Case had violent intent	
No	10
Yes	16
Unclear	6
Geographic location	
United States	28
United States or United Kingdom	1
Canada	1
Belgium	1
Germany	1

NOTES: Interviews represented 32 unique stories of radicalization, known as *cases*. We also assumed a binary gender distinction, drawn from interview data available, but recognize that the focal individuals may otherwise self-identify.

Table 3.2
Extreme Organization and Group Involvement

White Supremacist Organizations and Groups	Description	Islamic Extremist Organizations and Groups	Description
American Nazi Party	A political party for American Nazis	al Qaeda	A multinational militant Sunni Islamist group founded by Osama Bin Laden
Creativity Movement	A self-styled religious organization that heavily promotes what it sees as the inherent superiority and "creativity" of the white race	al Shabaab	An Islamist insurgency group based in Somalia
Daily Stormer	A website and message board that promote white supremacy and neo-Nazi causes	Anti-Christian Da'wah[a]	A nonmilitant ultraconservative sect of Islam
Hammerskins	An organized and ultraviolent skinhead neo-Nazi gang	ISIS	An ultraviolent terrorist organization known for establishing a self-styled and temporary caliphate, or Islamic homeland in Syria
KKK (e.g., Loyola White Nights, German KKK)	One of the oldest white supremacist groups, with a history of violence against minorities	Wahhabi[a]	An ultraorthodox Sunni Muslim sect
Heritage Front	A Canadian neo-Nazi white supremacist organization that existed between 1989 and 2005[b]		
National Alliance	A neo-Nazi organization that called for eradication of Jews and formation of an all-white homeland[c]		
National Democratic Party (Germany)	A far-right ultranationalist political party in Germany		
National Socialist Movement (NSM)	A large and prominent neo-Nazi organization known for provocative protests		
National Vanguard	A white nationalist, neo-Nazi organization		
Neo-Nazi	A broad label applied to groups known for hatred of Jews and other minorities and devotion to Adolf Hitler and Nazi Germany[d]		
Skinheads	A subculture known for shaved heads, tattoos, engagement in violent confrontations, and white power ideology		

Table 3.2—Continued

White Supremacist Organizations and Groups	Description	Islamic Extremist Organizations and Groups	Description
State Prison Skinheads	Prison based skinhead gang		
White Aryan Resistance	Network of white supremacist neo-Nazi skinheads formed by long-time white supremacist Tom Metzger[e]		
Youth for Western Civilization (YWC)	An ultraconservative student group that sought to defend Western civilization		
TWP	Neo-Nazi group that advocated for racially pure nation		

[a] These are religious sects rather than an extremist groups.

[b] Wikipedia, "Heritage Front," webpage, undated.

[c] Southern Poverty Law Center, "National Alliance," webpage, undated-a.

[d] Southern Poverty Law Center, "Neo-Nazi," webpage, undated-b.

[e] Anti-Defamation League, "White Aryan Resistance," webpage, undated.

Multiple former white supremacist cases were involved with the KKK (eight) and the NSM (nine), two of whom were involved with both. Four cases also mentioned being involved with skinheads, one of whom was also involved with the KKK and NSM.[1] Only two of the cases mentioned having been in the military, and a third had military training during adolescence.

Interview Process and Protocol

We conducted most (31) interviews over the phone, with five conducted in person during the annual meeting for one of our partner organizations. Interview duration ranged from 24 to 106 minutes, with a median duration of 61 minutes. In all cases, we digitally recorded interviews. We sent recordings to a professional transcription agency, which removed all names of people and places and returned a digital transcript to us using a secure file transfer process.[2] All respondents received a $50 gift card for their participation. All procedures were approved by RAND's HSPC.

---

[1] Involvement in radical organizations was described as ranging from minimal, such as attending events, to heavy involvement, including formal roles in an organization.

[2] All interviews were conducted in English, with a single exception; one interview respondent was more comfortable being interviewed in a foreign language, so we had a RAND team member with language fluency trans-

We spent the bulk of each interview having formers and family members tell us the story of their or their family members' radicalization and deradicalization ("in your own words, and from your own perspective"). To guide the narrative of radicalization and deradicalization, we asked respondents to begin with their or their family members' early lives, then discuss "major warning signals and turning points," followed by "attempts to intervene" made by family members, friends, or others (e.g., school officials, law enforcement). We went on to briefly discuss the focal individual's radical activities, then the process of deradicalization. To close out the interview, we asked all respondents about "missed opportunities"—in other words, things they think could have derailed the radicalization process or helped deradicalization occur more quickly. Finally, we asked respondents for any ideas they had for interventions (whether big or small) and whether they had anything else they would like to add. We used a similar protocol for both formers and family members, with minor modifications to refer to *you* (for interviews with formers) versus *them* or *your family member* (for family members); the full protocol is available in Appendix B.

Interview Analysis

After data collection was complete, we uploaded the transcripts to Dedoose, a team-based collaborative software program that facilitates data storage, management, analysis, and interpretation simultaneously across team members. The initial stage of analysis involved a grounded exploration of themes across the 36 interviews.[3] Two qualitative researchers from the team (Alina I. Palimaru and Sarah Weilant) coded eight transcripts (22 percent of the sample) independently, then met with the project leader (Ryan Andrew Brown) to discuss and reconcile codebook development, code definitions, and coding rules.[4] Codebook development was discussed in terms of balancing grounded findings with the study's scope and final report goal: practical recommendations relating to radicalization prevention and deradicalization support. The coders used a dedicated chat page in Microsoft Teams to check in regularly and discuss specific excerpts and coding strategies and amend code definitions in real time. On this chat page, coders flagged instances in which it was unclear how statements could be captured within the existing codebook. This typically resulted in either written comment exchanges following each post or ad hoc group conference calls. Decisions to

---

late the interview protocol into French and conduct the interview in French. The recorded interview was then transcribed in French and finally translated into English for analysis.

[3]   Gery W. Ryan and H. Russell Bernard, "Techniques to Identify Themes," *Field Methods*, Vol. 15, No. 1, 2003; H. Russell Bernard and Gery W. Ryan, "Text Analysis Qualitative and Quantitative Methods," in H. Russell Bernard, ed., *Handbook of Methods in Cultural Anthropology*, Walnut Creek, Calif.: AltaMira Press, 1998.

[4]   Kathleen M. MacQueen, Eleanor McLellan, Kelly Kay, and Bobby Milstein, "Codebook Development for Team-Based Qualitative Analysis," *Cultural Anthropology Methods*, Vol. 10, No. 2, 1998.

either expand existing definitions or add new codes were made considering the scope of the study. The coders also sought input from the full team of authors to help guide the coding process.

The codebook consisted of four main sections that follow a chronological perspective: *radicalization pathway* (i.e., the process by which a focal individual radicalized alone or was radicalized by others; it included two codes: warning signs and deliberate pursuit of an organization or messaging); *experience in the organization* (i.e., details about how an individual operated in the organization, with two codes: radical activities and radicalization impact); *deradicalization pathway* (i.e., the process by which a focal individual deradicalized alone or with help from others; it comprised ten codes, such as self-driven exit, successful interventions, and activism); and *practice and policy recommendations* (i.e., suggestions for practical solutions for preventing radicalization, precipitating deradicalization, and providing support after deradicalization; it included six codes, such as preventing radicalization, strategic communication, support groups, and mental health care). We also had a set of 45 floating descriptive codes that could be applied anywhere along the radicalization-deradicalization continuum, including turning point, missed opportunities, personal characteristics, shifts in social network, and community context. Although a formal check of intercoder reliability was not performed due to time constraints, our team is confident that the coders' deep involvement in both the codebook's development and its application mitigates against any dramatic variations in coding and interpretation.

Next, the team engaged in a detailed processing of the excerpts by theme in Excel, including summaries capturing the nuances of the thematic range, documenting the presence or absence of relevant attributes, and highlighting exemplary quotes. After coding was completed, the qualitative output was quantified using code frequencies (i.e., presence or absence of codes by interviewee and case) and code co-occurrence (i.e., the overlap or common occurrence of two or more codes in a given excerpt).

Notably, the content coded by the two coders was used slightly differently in each chapter, to accommodate analytic approaches suited to different topical focus of each chapter. For the background characteristics and vulnerability factors that we analyzed in Chapter Four, we made sure to examine all excerpts corresponding to each factor (e.g., substance use, family discord) and categorized each excerpt to determine whether the respondent drew an explicit or implicit link to radicalization or deradicalization. In some cases, we also categorized each excerpt by whether the factor under consideration applied to the preradicalization, radicalization, or deradicalization portion of the individual's life-course narrative. Two authors (Palimaru and Weilant) then aggregated findings to the level of the *case*, as some cases had more than one interview (e.g., the focal individual and spouse). For the cases with more than one interviewee, the narratives were largely aligned, with some complementary information that only the interviewee could provide, such as emotional reaction to certain events.

In Chapter Five, the very diverse and in some cases extensive narratives of the radicalization process demanded a slightly different (case-focused) approach. We began with Excel spreadsheets of formal coding output to generate ideas for summary codes describing core components of these narratives (e.g., propaganda, top-down recruitment). Then, one author (Todd C. Helmus) read each interview transcript in its entirety and categorized it by whether it included mention of these summary codes. The resultant analysis is a combination of formal coding in Dedoose and secondary sorting of individual cases using a *whole-person concept* to capture the diverse and complex narratives of radicalization. The written analysis of this content, including counts and use of quotes, was cross-checked and verified by the two coders (Palimaru and Weilant), as well as the lead author (Brown).

Chapter Six covers deradicalization processes. Our coding scheme covered these processes from a variety of perspectives—for example, "successful interventions" was one code, as was "role of institutions." Thus, the lead author (Brown) created a case summary table of common characteristics across codes pertaining to deradicalization, collecting and combining insights across codes in Excel and making note of relevant excerpts while doing so. This synthetic process also led to extensive code checking and auditing. Finally, Brown assembled insights at the case level to produce the text for Chapter Six.

Chapter Seven, covering respondents' insights into policies and practices to deter radicalization and encourage deradicalization, demanded yet a different analytic approach. In this case, one report author (Rajeev Ramchand) analyzed participant observations at the interview level, as we were interested in gathering insights not by radicalization case but by all respondents in our study. Furthermore, our analytic interest for this topic was to cover the broad diversity of recommendations rather than to document precise counts of the cases associated with each.

CHAPTER FOUR

Background Characteristics of Radical Extremists

As described in Chapter One, the conceptual framework guiding this study came from the CDC's socioecological framework for violence prevention, in which there are four levels of influence: individual, relationships (family and peers), community, and societal. In this chapter, we describe our sample using a similar framing.

Analysis of Interviews

Physical and Behavioral Health Challenges

Respondents sometimes described behavioral and physical health challenges faced by focal individuals. These are presented in Table 4.1, ordered from most to least common in the sample. We describe the content of discussions around these health challenges in the following sections.

Mental Health and Psychiatric Distress

U.S. estimates of mental illness prevalence among adults stand at roughly 20 percent.[1] In our sample, more than half of our cases (17: 12 white supremacists and five Islamic extremists) reported either diagnosed mental health issues or experiences of psychiatric or emotional distress. These included diagnosed disorders or disabilities, such as attention deficit hyperactivity disorder (ADHD), attention deficit disorder (ADD), bipolar disorder, and autism. They also included psychiatric or emotional issues, such as anxiety, a learning disability, depression, delusional thinking, uncontrollable or impulsive anger and violence, and suicidal ideation and attempts.

Importantly, mental health issues rarely seemed to be directly connected with radicalization or radical violence in our sample; rather, in these cases such challenges appeared to block other life-course opportunities or create vulnerability for being radicalized or being recruited into radical groups. For example, one former white supremacist explained: "I also have, like, a learning disorder. . . . The military won't take me. Like, I've been denied numerous jobs. . . . That's, like, something I've always struggled

---

[1]   National Institute of Mental Health, 2021.

Table 4.1
Summary of Personal Characteristics by Case

Health Challenge	White Supremacist	Islamic Extremist	Total
Mental health and psychiatric distress	12	5	17
Traumatic experiences	9	5	14
Substance use	10	3	13
Physical health	8	1	9

NOTE: The total sample consisted of 24 white supremacists and eight Islamic extremists (32 cases).

with in my life." Another former white supremacist with an autistic family member observed: "If you know anything about autism then you know, depending on what end of the spectrum they're on, they pick up on literally everything. You will most likely find that there are a lot of individuals that would fall on the autism spectrum involved with the far right."

One former white supremacist described sharing with a friend the emotional impact of bullying. That friend then started the focal individual on the radicalization pathway. As the focal individual recalled, the friend stated: "'I think I might be able to help.' And he pulled out a flyer from his bookbag, and he said, 'I belong to this organization that is a lobby group for people like us. You know, with European backgrounds.'" Also, another former white supremacist described how their anxiety as a child during an experience irrationally influenced their perceptions of race: "I have like strange anxiety and I can't stand anybody touching me. So, for me, . . . holding a kid's hand and my hand coming back all brown and blackish and I was convinced for the longest time that his blackness wore off on me."

Four cases described anger as a critical driver for joining radical groups or engaging in radical violence. In such cases, involvement in radical groups seemed to provide partial solutions to harmful early experiences with long-term emotional effects. For example, one former Islamic extremist was abused by a family member as a child and described how the lack of a family response was a push factor toward learning to protect themselves: "I became very, you know, angry at the fact that nobody did anything about it. Nobody could do anything about it. There was a pure—a sense of powerlessness. As I started to get older and more independent and more confident—so really from the age of 12, you know, when you kind of start to get over that hill . . . if anyone ever did that to me again, or my kids, or whatever, like I would destroy them." Meanwhile, one former white supremacist who was abandoned by a nonwhite parent described how violent impulses would activate suddenly during his involvement in a radical extremist group: "I was always the quiet and reserved guy who was pretty much the antithesis of what you'd expect until time came and something would just snap in my head where I felt like it was, you know, the fight-or-flight response."

Traumatic Experiences

We recognize that mental health issues can be associated with trauma.[2] Fourteen cases (nine white supremacists and five Islamic extremists) described traumatic experiences faced by focal individuals. Seven of these cases were ones in which mental health issues were also discussed. Accounts of traumatic events that focal individuals experienced included physical or sexual abuse, war trauma, accidents, and the death of a family member. Four focal individuals experienced or witnessed traumatic events before joining an extreme group and linked these experiences in some way to radicalization. For example, one focal individual described joining a radical organization as a way to cope with losing several friends to suicide. Meanwhile, six cases described how traumatic experiences led to psychological changes that created greater vulnerability to radicalization later in life. For example, one former white supremacist described how their views on race and pathway to radicalization were influenced by a traumatic event when they were younger; "My oldest brother was shot by an African American man. . . . So my process of whenever I thought about . . . minorities in general, I thought of guns." Finally, three cases mentioned PTSD and traumatic experiences due to violence experienced while in the radical organization. As one former white supremacist noted, referring to the culture in the organization they were involved with: "There's so much trauma and death and destruction and wreckage of lives."

Substance Use

Thirteen focal individuals (ten white supremacists and three Islamic extremists) described using alcohol or other drugs, including marijuana (others might have used alcohol or other drugs but did not include them in their personal narratives). Of these, three participants' substance use seemed limited to adolescent years. For the rest, substance use continued throughout their radicalization (two cases), their experience in the radical organization (four cases), or both (three cases). For most of those who started heavy drinking in their teens and continued into adulthood, substance use was typically preceded by being bullied at school, parental divorce, or other childhood trauma. One former white supremacist pointed out that, while in the organization, members may feel a lot of stress associated with poverty or the need to hide their radical identity, saying, for example, that "alcoholism in the movement is a huge, huge problem." Another former white supremacist said: "I was using illegal drugs. All of these other guys were using illegal drugs. I was partying with some of them, so I saw it personally." No respondents identified substance use as the primary driver of their radicalization, although former radicals described engaging in violence fueled by substance use.

---

[2] Angela Sweeney, Beth Filson, Angela Kennedy, Lucie Collinson, and Steve Gillard, "A Paradigm Shift: Relationships in Trauma-Informed Mental Health Services," *BJPsych Advances*, Vol. 24, No. 5, 2018.

Physical Health

Nine cases (one Islamic extremist and eight white supremacists) discussed the role of physical health. Five cases made an explicit connection between physical health and radicalization, including one white supremacist who was an amputee and justified certain radical views: "I was aware that even the Nazis would go after the handicapped and so that didn't bother me because modern National Socialism was about white separatism. It wasn't really necessarily about genocide for anybody." There were also two instances in which experiences of being bullied in grade school and high school due to their physical appearance had a lasting impact on former white supremacists. One who had a facial anomaly stated: "I was the weird kid that was bullied with the weird clothes that doesn't fit in anywhere . . . with a crooked face."

Two cases described physical health issues related to military experiences. One white supremacist attempted to join the military but was denied due to a physical issue and described that experience as a "letdown," a time when they started to seek out members of an extreme group. For the other, a military injury led them to a drug addiction and interactions with other individuals with substance use disorders who were in extreme groups. Physical health was also a driver for deradicalization (discussed in more detail in Chapter Six) in two former white supremacists' cases—for one a cancer diagnosis turned them toward religion, which in turn helped deradicalize them, while another had medical complications due to drug use, which was a tipping point for their family members to intervene and help them on a different path.

Criminal History and Multicausal Psychological Underpinnings of Violence

Past research has identified criminal history as a way to predict engagement in violent activities among those in radical organizations, especially when paired with mental health or other psychological challenges.[3] In our sample, we identified only four cases that mentioned having a criminal history or arrest record before starting to radicalize. Of these cases, three out of four also engaged in violence while in radical organizations (or had violent intent).

We also looked at *accumulated influence* for the 15 cases in which violent intent or violent activity were present. Ten of these 15 cases had two or more of the following: prior criminal history, mental health or psychological distress, trauma or PTSD, and substance use. For the remaining 16 cases in which violent intent was either not present or it was impossible to determine from the interviews, only five of them had two or more of the factors listed above (criminal history, mental health, trauma, and substance use).

---

[3]   Michael A. Jensen, Anita Atwell Seate, and Patrick A. James, "Radicalization to Violence: A Pathway Approach to Studying Extremism," *Terrorism and Political Violence*, Vol. 32, No. 5, July 2020.

Family and Community Context

In the following sections, we describe social and community-level factors, including socioeconomic circumstances, family context, and neighborhood environment.

Financial Challenges

Twenty-two cases (19 white supremacists and three Islamic extremists) described financial hardship in some way. Six focal individuals described financial hardship as part of their life experiences but did not make explicit links between this and radicalization or deradicalization. However, seven cases did make this explicit link. For one former Islamic extremist, poverty meant that her parents could not afford to pay for her therapy when, as a child, she struggled with isolation and being bullied: "When I was young, none of that was available because my parents didn't have money, I didn't have money, and they didn't believe in that stuff because they weren't educated. . . . If I had the role models and the supervision, like the good kind, I would have seen a therapist or a counselor about the bullying and then how that isolated me, you know."

Meanwhile, a former white supremacist described experiencing financial difficulties as an adult, which compounded racial perceptions and pushed him toward radicalization: "When I got out [of the military], the economy was so bad, it took me a while to find a job. So I was constantly on the computer looking for jobs and then I'd get bored and you apply to the same job 100 times, like a cycle. They're up on the job board, then they disappear, then they pop back up a few days later and you reapply. . . . And I was like, yeah, getting out [of the military] with 11 years in, I should be able to get a job on base, no problem, as a contractor. Nah, that didn't happen. So, I decided to blame my problems on somebody else and say, 'Oh, it's the black people's fault.'"

Family Discord and Distress

Case narratives often described stressful circumstances in the family, including heavy substance use by other family members, abuse, neglect, and strained or broken family relationships. Several focal individuals experienced alcoholism (four cases) and substance dependence or drug use (two cases) by family members and unpleasant experiences linked with this. For example, one former white supremacist explained, "My father's drinking made life really difficult for my mom and that hurt me, because I could tell my mom was suffering." Five focal individuals also experienced physical, emotional, or sexual abuse by a family member.[4] Three of these five cases were categorized as someone with violent intent during their careers as violent extremists. Notably, however, there were also cases in which individuals did not describe abusive experiences, did describe being in loving families, and also had violent intent.

In seven cases, focal individuals experienced either the death of a parent or having only one parent present in their lives. However, any links between losing a parent (or parental absence) and radicalization were either unclear or highly varied. One former

---

[4] One of those cases referred to abuse of one parent toward another.

white supremacist in a single-parent home explained: "My siblings had left the nest and I was the only one left because I was so much younger. And I'd say seventh grade, maybe, Mom went back to work. So I had free rein. There wasn't a lot of follow-through as far as discipline is concerned." In one case, the death of a parent was described as a turning point in behavior, when an individual started bullying others and fighting, while another said that it triggered their deradicalization process.

Family Extremism

There is limited research on the link between radicalization and having a family history of extremism.[5] Seven former white supremacists described some relationship between their own radicalization and family roots. Only one case described direct family involvement in radical organizations, a former white supremacist who suggested that their father might have been a member of the KKK: "As far as I know, while I was younger he was never part of any kind of, like, organized radical groups, but at the same time, he would make comments like he either had been involved in or was friends with people that were in the Klan back in the day and made it sound like it was an OK thing." During their own radicalization, three former white supremacists described becoming increasingly interested in their German family history, including one grandparent with German heritage whose "racist tendencies" influenced the family who are "still racially motivated by things that they do and say." Additionally, three former white supremacists noted that racism was acceptable in their households; one had a father they described as an "armchair racist," while another described their father's racists comments going unquestioned in the family, and the third described both of their parents encouraging violence against Muslims after the events of September 11, 2001: "Especially right after it, it was just like, 'We should bomb 'em, annihilate them all. Like, this is ridiculous what they're doing,' just typical kind of Fox News talking points, I would say, more or less. Because my parents didn't start watching Fox News until 9/11 happened and then as soon as that happened, it's been Fox News."

Neighborhood Demographics, Marginalization, and Discrimination

Sixteen focal individuals (13 white supremacists and three Islamic extremists) talked about feeling victimized, stigmatized, or marginalized where they grew up or lived and how this contributed to their radicalization.[6] Most of the examples cited exposure to African American or Latinx populations and other nonwhite groups in neighborhoods and schools, which often resulted in a sense of social isolation. As this former white supremacist explained: "As I got older I was going to schools, and I'm in [city], and the school that I was attending was about 80 percent Cambodian, Laotian, and black. And

---

[5]   Gary LaFree, Michael A. Jensen, Patrick A. James, and Aaron Safer-Lichtenstein, "Correlates of Violent Political Extremism in the United States," *Criminology*, Vol. 56, No. 2, 2018.

[6]   Conversely, in Chapter Six we illustrate how exposure to demographic and cultural diversity helped some focal individuals to deradicalize.

I was one of maybe three white kids in the entire school. And I was going there and I always felt very alienated, very different from everyone else."

Other narratives hinted at some of the underlying mechanisms (e.g., perceived lack of job opportunities, the effect of public discourse on race relations in everyday life) that may link exposure to diversity with radicalization:

> So I'm about halfway through my high school, the military moved us to [location], which I would say is probably about 98 percent black. It was like culture shock going from all white to all black. And there was little things with, like, I wouldn't get jobs because I wasn't the right colors to apply there. My dad had a heart attack and a couple of strokes, so he went to rehab and they were like, "Well, it's not that you don't qualify but, really, I mean you're white, how much problem could you really have?" So that kind of firmed it up where it was like, Jesus Christ!

Similarly, one former Islamic extremist described the racism they experienced in their neighborhood from other racial minority groups, which filled them with resentment: "I always think that a lot of racism, and even discrimination not even from some white people but from other, other minority groups for being [South Asian], for being Muslim. Things that I didn't even choose but I was, you know, and things I didn't even like. But I was still hated for those things."

Conclusion

Our study of 32 cases of extremists was heterogenous and covered a broad range of former white and Islamic extremists who were involved with a range of organizations. We did not ask specifically about hypothesized factors associated with extremism but noted when individual, family, or environmental (including community, social, and cultural) factors were described during extremists' accounts. Fewer than half the sample explicitly framed personal substance use, trauma, and physical health as drivers of radicalization, and though mental health and financial hardship were mentioned in many cases, they were inconsistently linked directly to extremism. Fewer than half of respondents talked about family-level attributes, such as discord and distress or a history of family extremism. The community and broader social context was discussed in fewer than half of cases. Such discussions predominantly centered on feeling marginalized or discriminated against because of political and cultural changes or neighborhood demographic makeup.

CHAPTER FIVE

Pathways to Radicalization

This chapter covers the stories of how focal individuals in our sample were radicalized, highlighting major processes that interviewees described as pertinent to radicalization. The radicalization processes described in the 32 cases represent a heterogenous mix of background factors, critical events, and recruitment processes.

Analysis of Interviews

Through aggregating coded excerpts and reading through full interview transcripts to sort radicalization trajectories into types (see "Interview Analysis" in Chapter Three for more detail), we identified the following common themes on the radicalization pathway:

- dramatic life-course reorienting events that create vulnerability or openness to radicalization
- consumption of extremist propaganda
- exhibition of outward signs of radicalization (observable by others)
- top-down recruitment into radical organization
- bottom-up or individual "searching" for radical involvement
- moves from less- to more-extreme organizations
- rewards of being involved in radical organizations.

The prevalence of these themes in white supremacist and Islamic extremist cases is illustrated in Table 5.1.

Presence of a Reorienting Event

Drawing on the social movement literature, Wiktorowicz argued that an individual must be willing to be exposed to the radical views of terror organizations or peers.[1] He

---

[1]   Quintan Wiktorowicz, *Islamic Activism: A Social Movement Theory Approach*, Bloomington: Indiana University Press, 2004.

Table 5.1
Key Radicalization Themes Addressed in This Chapter (by case)

	White Supremacists	Islamic Extremists	Total
Presence of a reorienting event	15	4	19
Experience with propaganda	12	4	16
Showing signs of radicalization	6	4	10
Top-down recruitment	4	3	7
Bottom-up joining	15	3	18
Graduating to more-extreme organizations	9	1	10
Initial rewards	17	2	19

NOTE: The total sample consisted of 24 white supremacists and eight Islamic extremists (32 cases).

highlighted that an individual psychological crisis can shake "certainty in previously accepted beliefs and renders an individual more receptive to the possibility of alternative views and perspectives."[2] In reviewing this study's transcripts and applied codes, it became apparent that such a reorienting event took place in at least a small subset of participants.[3]

We observed this phenomenon in four Islamic extremist cases and seven white supremacist cases. Across many of these instances, the striking resemblance was that of a precipitating event and emotional reaction and then a new outlook or direction that made room for extremist ideology or participation. For one former Islamic extremist, a gun-possession charge served as a stimulating event and led him to "start looking around to try to better himself or try to improve his life and his lifestyle." His answer was a conversion to Islam and then a turn toward radicalization and violence. Another converted and then radicalized after a suicide attempt. Another former Islamic extremist reported that his life came "crashing down before [his] eyes" when a relative caught him hosting a rowdy house party. "I'm humiliated, I'm embarrassed, I have been shamed and guilt-tripped into thinking that I have done something so heinous," he observed. "I panicked psychologically, and looked back into my cultural experience, and think to myself, the only way that I'm going to fix this is to get religious."

---

[2]   Wiktorowicz, 2004. This phenomenon is also addressed in prior research, with Jensen noting that "two conditions—cognitive frame alignment and community crisis—are 'near' necessary conditions for radicalization to violent extremism." See Jensen et al., 2016, p. 71.

[3]   In Chapter Four, we described a variety of life insults and stressors, many of which respondents did not link to radicalization (or made only indirect connections). Here, we focus on focus on dramatic (sometimes traumatic) events with an explicit, direct link to "conversion" to extremism (which is sometimes a final step in a series).

For white supremacists, precipitating events included rejection by the military, which led one individual to seek out skinheads at a local nightclub; a friend's suicide, which led to a career change that brought someone in direct contact with white supremacists; an extended stint of unemployment during which boredom led to exposure to extremist right-wing propaganda; and a rape by a Hispanic male that led to a "different mindset" and direction in life.

One individual took a shot at success, getting his own apartment and taking a management training job in a nearby big city: "And it kind of felt like a scene in a movie when the protagonist is finally going to get his big chance, his big shot." It all fell apart. He was demoted at work, failed to make friends, returned to his mom's house, and sought treatment for depression:

> I . . . was just living in hell . . . and anything that was antireligious kind of appealed to me, so I kind of got in this mindset of well, what else is wrong? What else have I been lied to about? And . . . something about the whole antisocial nature of [the Third Reich] appealed to me. . . . [I]f I'm so smart and I still can't even make it, something's screwed up with the world. . . . And I started checking out different websites and just kind of looking into some . . . propaganda on some of those ideas.

For some focal individuals, certain experiences with racial minorities could be described as reorienting events. In these cases, idiosyncratic and certainly nonrepresentative events produced a cognitive and emotional reaction that led them toward extremism. One individual, who experienced a lifetime of flirting with racist ideology, experienced a tipping of the scales when he discovered that a black man who was selling him drugs was sleeping with his sister-in-law. The very day of his discovery, he called a white supremacist organization's hotline and joined the group. Others described early childhood experiences, interpretation of which eventually pushed them over the edge. One recalled having "dirty hands" after holding the hand of a black child, and another recalled that, when he was a child, a black individual shot his brother. Other examples that participants noted included the presence of race riots in their towns, feelings of alienation experienced at a mostly black school, and even negative perceptions of the growing Black Lives Matter movement.

Consumption of Propaganda

Overall, 21 cases described the consumption of propaganda in their journeys to extremism. Islamic extremists accounted for five of these cases and white supremacists the remaining 16. Prominent media for this propaganda consisted of social media and the internet, music, and books or literature.

Social Media and the Internet

For the five Islamic extremists, who tended to be younger than the white supremacists, online exposure to propaganda was the most commonly referenced propaganda source, being present in four cases. These individuals reportedly saw religious sermons, most notably by the famed and now deceased Jihadi idealogue Anwar al Awlaki, or videos depicting attacks against Muslims.

A relative of one deceased Islamic extremist observed that his religious school introduced him to videos depicting Muslims under attack. The relative exclaimed: "Of course they're appalling and for anybody that cares about children they would tug at the heartstrings. I could see easily how somebody could draw you into believing. . . . We're immortal, we want to take a stand, we want to make a difference." Another likewise noted that "those were the images that came to our children's homes. So there were really recruiters on the internet who sent messages, links to persecutions against Muslims in China for example. . . . And then young people said, . . . 'We're not going to wait for someone to save us.'"

Online propaganda was also common for right-wing extremists, being present in nine individual cases. Specific modes and outlets included YouTube videos, 4chan, the Daily Stormer and the Stormfront websites, and even old-fashioned chatrooms that were prominent in the late 1980s. One former white supremacist stated that perusing the Daily Stormer led to participating in that site's local online book club. Another individual described how his exposure to online propaganda led him to see the "small kernels of truth" that took him in a "really wrong direction." He continued: "I guess [this] is kind of what propaganda is. And so it kind of was just really a perfect storm. . . . It just kind of took it in a really dark direction."

Music

Music also plays a prominent role in right-wing extremism. White power music, in particular, promotes white nationalism and white supremacist themes in genres that range from rock 'n' roll to country music, and music is a major part of neo-Nazi skinhead culture.[4] At least four cases highlighted the presence of punk rock as highly formative. One individual who went on to join the KKK described how he was "recruited by the music." A schoolyard friend gave him a cassette tape, and, as he observed: "I was like . . . , how do they know me? How is that happening? . . . It was loud rock music and screaming voices that . . . I liked so much. All of a sudden it had a message, too. I was hooked, that was my thing." He observed that "the music got more radical, more hateful. So I started fitting in with this skinhead music. . . . At the age of 15, I wanted to get to know skinheads, that was the people that I only knew from the music, do they really exist? Where are they?" Another individual described how the music's reference

---

[4]   See, for example, John M. Cotter, "Sounds of Hate: White Power Rock and Roll and the Neo-Nazi Skinhead Subculture," *Terrorism and Political Violence*, Vol. 11, No. 2, 1999; Anti-Defamation League, *The Sounds of Hate: The White Power Music Scene in the United States in 2012*, New York, 2012; Robert Futrell, Pete Simi, and Simon Gottschalk, "Understanding Music in Movements: The White Power Music Scene," *Sociological Quarterly*, Vol. 47, No. 2, 2006.

to a "broken home" and "poor family" led him to conclude that the music was "very relatable." He observed, "It's like, they understand me, you know."

Books and Literature

Six cases highlighted the importance of books and literature. At least three individuals described themselves growing up as German military history buffs. One individual, whose fascination started with a grandfather who fought for the German Third Reich, began reading German military history. He borrowed Adolf Hitler's *Mein Kampf* from his local library; from there, he came across a book by David Lane called *88 Precepts*, the title of which refers to a symbolic term for *Heil Hitler*. Inside that book, he found the descriptions of and contact information for right-wing extremist groups that ultimately led him to join the NSM. Another individual highlighted the importance of Third Reich books, including *The Life and Death of Adolf Hitler* by James Giblin. He noted, "in feeding my curiosity, I only became more obsessed."

Joining Extremist Organizations

One question that arises is how people, often by this point already holding extremist views, make formal ties with extremist organizations. This issue of making a connection with the group was not a focus of background literature review. It is important, though, as understanding this connection pathway may shed light on mitigation strategies.

One approach is through the impetus of the extremist organization. Previous international research on radicalization highlights the oftentimes formal efforts by extremist outfits to find and recruit new members. Al Qaeda recruiters in Saudi Arabia, for example, invited potential recruits to attend seemingly informal gatherings in homes that were carefully calibrated to radicalize and ultimately enlist new members.[5] Other approaches are less formal, relying on membership recruiting friends and family members.[6] Alternatively, in a process most famously described by Sageman,[7] people radicalize on their own or commonly in peer social circles and only then, on their own initiative, make formal connections with extremist organizations.[8] We refer

[5]   Thomas Hegghammer, "Terrorist Recruitment and Radicalization in Saudi Arabia," *Middle East Policy*, Vol. 13, No. 4, 2006.

[6]   Edwin Bakker, *Jihadi Terrorists in Europe: Their Characteristics and the Circumstances in Which They Joined the Jihad; An Exploratory Study*, Clingendael: Netherlands Institute of International Relations, December 2006.

[7]   Marc Sageman, *Leaderless Jihad: Terror Networks in the Twenty-First Century*, Philadelphia: University of Pennsylvania Press, 2008.

[8]   Here, we do not take issue with the infamous debate by terrorism scholars Bruce Hoffman and Marc Sageman, who contested whether it was such extremist organizations as al Qaeda that represented the greatest security threat or self-radicalized and leaderless "bunches of guys." The vast majority of participants in our sample considered themselves members of an extremist organization. The issue is thus not one of organization versus no organization but how people make contact with the organization and the organization's role in that recruitment

to the former, recruitment-driven process as *top-down* and the latter, member-driven process as *bottom-up.*

Top-Down (Deliberate Outreach) Recruitment

In our sample, formal recruiters were mentioned in three cases. One individual was recruited into ISIS by a charismatic street preacher. The recruit's close relative noted that this preacher was

> someone who did a lot of damage with his speeches, with his sermons . . . and started to talk about strong religion. It was like an orgasm. The young people felt like they existed. They had more power, because there was someone who represented them. And so that's the notion among young people of belonging to a strong group and that group was not a group of criminals or offenders. It was an ideological group.

In another case, a mother discovered that a teacher at her son's religious school was a recruiter for al Shabaab. The teacher was arrested by the FBI, and it was apparent that he so transfixed his students that her son and a number of other classmates attended the recruiter's court hearing after his arrest by federal investigators. Another parent suggested that a recruiter, who was being watched by the FBI, was able to recruit her son.

Top-down recruitment amid white supremacists appeared more informal by contrast. One individual described confiding in a friend about the bullying and abuse they were receiving in school. And the friend, offering to help, pulled out a flyer and said: "I belong to this organization that is a lobby for people like us, you know with European backgrounds." The friend handed out some flyers on the group. The individual recruited read the material thinking: "Oh my gosh, this is amazing. Like this is the answer." A similar approach defined one focal individual's entry into the KKK and another's entry into the prison-based white supremacist Creativity Movement. Reflecting a possibly more formal approach, another individual reportedly disappeared for six months and returned an avowed member of a right-wing extremist group. His friend thought that he was under the sway of recruiters.

Bottom-Up Entry

In bottom-up entry, radicalization occurs without the assistance of a recruiter, and individuals seek out participation in extremist activities and organizations of their own accord. Only a few cases of Islamic extremism were classified as bottom-up. One occurred when an individual radicalized by family and friends at home connected to extremist activities when she married an extremist she met online. In another case, a young Muslim was caught by a relative throwing a raucous house party, and then felt

---

process. For more on the Hoffman-Sageman debate, see Elaine Sciolino and Eric Schmitt, "A Not Very Private Feud over Terrorism," *New York Times*, June 8, 2008.

compelled to get religious. His answer was to seek out membership in a nonpolitical fundamentalist group in Pakistan. Upon return home, he reached out to a local Islamic group advocating violent extremism that had coincidentally tried unsuccessfully to recruit him two years earlier in his mosque: "But now that I had now gone over and I had this experience, I came back, I actually went to them. And there was actually a joke that, you know, we came to you so many times and like, you didn't have the time of day for us. And now suddenly, you're here."

For white supremacists, however, the cases more clearly reverberate as bottom-up. With their constitutional protections, white supremacists and other right-wing groups are free to publicize their activities and offer open opportunities to connect. Barbecues, cookouts, and other public events, for example, offer opportunities to prospective recruits to check out the organization and make connections. One participant in our study noted that her boyfriend invited her to an NSM barbecue at which she hit it off with one of its leaders. Another reported that he "gathered up the family and . . . drove to Georgia from North Carolina" and participated in a small NSM cookout rally. He continued, "And we met them all and they were really welcoming." Another went to the Minnesota State Fair and connected with a white identity group that in turn offered him information for other local extremist groups. After requesting information by mail, he settled on the NSM, which most aligned with his support for the German National Socialist Movement.

Others reached out online or even by telephone. After concluding (from watching an episode of the History Channel show *Gangland*) that the Klan was best for him, one individual reached out to several KKK outfits he found on the internet. He received a response from only one such organization, and he was able to connect in person at a subsequent rally event. Another impulsively called a KKK "hotline" after learning that his sister-in-law was sleeping with a black man.

Three individuals even went so far as to start their own extremist organizations. In one case, a prison inmate formed his own skinhead gang as a form of protection against black separatist groups operating in the prison. Although the individual has since left extremism, his group has continued to grow and expand. Another started his own white supremacy group after being dissatisfied with existing options. And another reported a "thrilling" experience with white power music, and he started his own skinhead gang and band. As he retells it:

> The band was like the rallying point that drew more pissed-off white kids to our crew, and within a couple months we went from three or four to ten to 20. And by the summer of '88 . . . we were getting national attention from other skinhead groups and other neo-Nazi groups, and all along we were like fighting constantly. We're attacking people in the street. We're drinking profusely. The more we radiated hate and violence into the world, the more the world reflected it back to us.

Graduating to More-Formal or More-Extreme Organizations

We also identified a number of cases in which individuals progressed or graduated from one extremist organization to another, often a more extreme outfit. In at least four cases, negative experiences or conflicts within one group led an individual to leave and join another. One individual who reported making friends in a local book club that was affiliated with the Daily Stormer website ultimately left and transitioned to the more formal TWP, a neo-Nazi group that advocated for racially pure nations, because he found many in the book club engaging in "mean-spirited jokes and drinking and very little else. It wasn't productive." Another was participating in the anti-immigration student group YWC when, after experiencing problems, he decided to start his own extremist organization.[9] In addition to intellectual disagreements, he observed: "Really, I wasn't impressed by anyone. I thought they were all either charlatans or dumb or just had a really backwards ideology, or all of the above. So I got really turned off by the movement in general for a long time." And another disliked the Loyal White Knights, an offshoot of the KKK, because she found them to be a "disorganized band of people" who "didn't have it together." So, she left the group and joined the NSM, one of the largest and most prominent neo-Nazi hate groups in the United States, which she felt she had more in common with.

In a final category, one individual reported that attempts to quit extremism only led him to a more extremist outfit. He noted that he disliked participation in a skinhead gang and so quit and tried to go to college. But he was still dressing and looking like a skinhead and was easily sighted by another skinhead gang near campus. It was this group that sought him out and ultimately recruited him into the NSM. And that participation in the NSM led to a more political and nationalistic kind of radicalization.

Five other cases appeared to graduate up to a more extreme form of radical group. The one case of Islamic extremism that applies here involves the case of the Western Muslim who traveled to Pakistan to participate in a group that, admittedly, was a nonpolitical and nonmilitant Muslim group (and thus not an extremist organization). During this time, he ran into more-militant circles of this group. As he recounts:

> And so they listened to me, and then he [a member of the group] says, "Well, if you want to change the world, you do it with this." And he picked up the AK-47. I mean, these guys had weapons displayed in front of them like they were ready to go. Now, this Muslim kid, from [the West], seeking this new religious identity, having this Army cadet militancy background—when I see these guys, they are everything that I am looking for in one. Right? It all comes to a focal point, right here. So I became completely enamored by them. I said that these guys are like the people I read about in the books.

---

[9]   The name of the organization is redacted to maintain participant anonymity.

The experience proved crucial when he returned home in motivating him to look up a local Islamic group that advocated violent attacks. Similarly, a white supremacist described his graduation from the neo-Nazi group National Vanguard to the NSM by highlighting that the latter "seemed more official" and that "to get our message out there, we need to be extreme. And the extreme is to go back to the '40s and then use the swastika and use all the marching and stuff." Still another transitioned out of a militant punk rock band to a group of skinheads, describing the latter, in glowing terms, as "the hardest motherfuckers I ever saw in my life"; he was giddy that they shook hands with him "straight up." Another case, however, just "graduated." After participating in a skinhead gang for four years, he turned 18 and was able to join the NSM. He attended a rally and submitted an "application."

Initial Rewards of Participation

What did people like about participating in an extremist group? In this section, we highlight some of the positive initial reactions once individuals became actively engaged in extremism.

First, 14 cases (12 white supremacists and two Islamic supremacists) commented on how, upon joining their radical organizations, they found family and friendship. One observed that, in hanging out in online chatrooms: "[I would] stay on there all night and then started making friends there, meeting up and then that was my kind of only friends." Another noted: "I never had been a part of a group that was as tight as [radical group], even though there was a lot of infighting in it. So you go to those rallies and everyone's your brother, everyone's extremely cool, friendly." And another observed: "People talked, they communicated, they formed close bonds and were not only just members of an organization but they were friends. And you had your own little society going on inside there as opposed to when you leave you're kind of on your own because most of them don't want to have anything to do with you once you've left the organization." Another former white supremacist noted: "Yeah, I alienated myself from my high school or friends in college, but then I made new friends in the movement. . . . And then I was meeting people by going to conferences and building those relationships. I mean, I really just traded one family and one set of friends for another family and other set of friends that accepted me more than my own flesh and blood did and respected me more, honestly. . . . It was exciting. It was fun. I had more friends than I knew what to do with."

Three participants found the social milieu of the white supremacy groups particularly attractive, given the absence of social connections before joining. One noted the attraction of being valued. He noted that he was displaced from his community and not feeling that he was "significant to anybody": "To have someone say, 'We see you. We see the problem. We believe you can help fix it and we need you.' And to give that kind of messaging was just, to me at that time, just absolutely intoxicating. And I just went all in really fast." Another reported: "I just found people of like mind, most of whom were around my age, and built a new subculture and community and like pseudofamily that was far more organic and involved in each other's lives than the traditional, nuclear, American family that's really just like a broken, decaying husk of what a family is supposed to be." Still another former white supremacist noted: "It was like we found family. I mean, my own family had cut me off because of other reasons because they didn't like my ex-wife. So I didn't really have family at that point. I didn't have many friends. I was pretty much living across the country. And we met the [radical group] guys and they were so welcoming and they were so like me that it was, like, all right, this is family right here and we joined."

Other participants highlighted the power, meaning, and affirmation they received from participating in extremism. Three individuals highlighted power. One noted how "people switch the side of the street when they see you. . . . It was a great feeling, even thinking back it was a great feeling." Another described a family member's experience as going from feeling undervalued and weak "to feeling that sense of power and control."

Others were entranced by their newfound mission in life. One Islamic extremist noted: "We all feel like we're fighting for God and God is holy and righteous and good; it made us feel special. It made us feel like where, it's good, you know it's very black and white." A white supremacist felt as if he "had really discovered the truth and . . . had to let everybody know." And another felt like a "superhero." He continued: "Even though half the white race doesn't understand what you're doing, in your mind, you're going to save them. You're like Superman and you're doing something good and noble." Meanwhile, the family member of one former (now deceased) Islamic extremist described how one charismatic convert to Islam created an "orgiastic" sense of group identity through his speeches and public worship, including periodic exhortations of *Allahu Akbar*: "They felt like they existed, young people. They had more power, because there was someone who represented them. And so that's the notion among young people of belonging to a strong group and that group was not a group of criminals or offenders."

Finally, another three focal individuals described the experience as one of affirmation. One noted how, in contrast to a drunk father calling him insulting names, a man he met from a white supremacist group "was the opposite." "He told me I was an intelligent young man, that I had leadership qualities, and that they needed people like me." Another noted how, although miserable, he refused to leave because he was "revered" and had a "huge inflated identity in the movement." He went on to explain, "I was kind of legendary [in radical group], and in the real world I was just an alcoholic, high school dropout who was dealing drugs to pay his bills and kept moving back into mom's house and had a tendency to drink 'til he passed out and pissed all over himself."

External Signs of Radicalization

We paid particularly close attention to examples in which our cases displayed observable signs in the relatively early phases of their radicalization, before they came out publicly and or committed some irreversible act.

In four cases of Islamic extremists, the interviewed family members or focal individuals reported externally observable signs of individual radicalization. Two of these cases were converts to Islam for whom changes in behavior were obvious to non-Muslim family members and friends. In one case, an individual converted to Islam after being arrested for possession of guns and marijuana. He soon became more "serious" and ceased being his "laughing self." He got rid of his possessions, including his furniture and car. He even abandoned his dog in the wilderness, a sign that his father took that "something was wrong." He also "stopped coming home" and acted secretively regarding his newfound social network. In the capstone of changes, he informed his family of his intention to study the Arabic language in a relatively unstable part of the Middle East, a trip that ultimately cemented his transition to violent extremism. Another individual who converted wanted his mother to read related material and expressed interest in traveling to Saudi Arabia to learn the Quran. He also watched videocassette tapes of extremist preachers, although his mother was unaware of the extremist nature of this content.

Changes in behavior were also observed for two Islamic extremists who were not religious converts. In one case, an individual reportedly became "extremely quiet" and "started to spend more time at the mosque," including "sleeping over." Another "started wearing religious clothing associated with extreme Islam and voicing more-extreme ideas to family, telling [their] own grandmother they would go to hell."

For white supremacists, it often appeared that early and direct signs of right-wing ideology were visible to others. In one case a focal individual reported that in high school he created a minute-long video on Nazis and notably did not denounce them in any way. Another high schooler mounted Nazi SS and Confederate flags on his bedroom wall. His mother was reportedly ignorant of such symbols at the time. Others reported racist language in schoolyard fights or the wearing of swastika jewelry. Finally, another reported a series of events that were ultimately not noticed by his mother. These included being removed from a school field trip for wearing "radical clothes" and lying to his mother about it, drafting Hitler-themed comics, and making racist taunts during schoolyard fights.

Conclusion

Our respondents provided detailed, complex, and varied accounts of their own and their family members' radicalization journeys. The key to radicalization seemed to be a dramatic life event that created new openness and vulnerability to radicalization. Radicalization was clearly multicausal, with contributing factors ranging from personal trauma to national media events. Consumption of propaganda was a notable feature of the radicalization process, including messaging on social media and the internet. Focal individuals described two primary processes for joining radical groups; some cases involved top-down recruitment (most common among Islamic extremist organizations), while others reflected a bottom-up entry, whereby individuals sought out messaging and organizations on their own (more prevalent among white supremacists). Some respondents mentioned a progression through multiple, and gradually more extremist, organizations, a process driven primarily by disillusionment with the effectiveness of some organizations. Importantly, participants shared their perceived external signs of radicalization, such as departures from usual behaviors, personality changes, and manifest display of symbols (e.g., SS flags, swastika jewelry).

CHAPTER SIX

Deradicalizing and Leaving Extremist Organizations

This chapter covers the stories of how focal individuals in our sample deradicalized or left extremist organizations.

Analysis of Interviews

Current Status

Using an inductive process, our data coders classified our 32 focal individuals into four categories that describe the degree to which the individuals had established distance from radical organizations and beliefs. These four categories (listed below) resulted from combinations of the following three factors: (1) whether individuals had exited the radical organization they were part of (*exited*), (2) whether individuals had undergone a cognitive and emotional shift away from radical beliefs (*deradicalized*), and (3) whether individuals were currently involved in trying to deradicalize others (*activist*).[1] The four resulting categories and the counts of focal individuals in each category are reported in Table 6.1.

Thus, most of our sample (20 out of 32 cases) had exited a radical organization and had undergone a process of psychological (i.e., shift in mindset) and social (i.e., distancing themselves from other radicals) deradicalization. Out of these 20 cases, most of them (12 cases) were also activists, currently engaged in deradicalizing others. Meanwhile, six of our cases had exited a radical organization but were still undergoing cognitive and emotional deradicalization. These individuals sometimes expressed a lack of regret over prior involvement or even indicated that their ideological views had not changed.

Of those who had not exited and not deradicalized, four were Islamic extremists who had died in Jihadist military campaigns or after being imprisoned (in these cases, we spoke with friends and family of these individuals). Two were white supremacists; of these, one was an acquaintance with whom our interviewee had lost contact and

---

[1] After developing these categories, our two coders (Palimaru and Weilant) separately categorized all 32 cases and resolved any discrepancies.

Table 6.1
Current Status of Focal Individuals

Type of Individual Who Intervened	White Supremacist	Islamic Extremist	Total
Exited, deradicalized, and activist	10	2	12
Exited and deradicalized	7	1	8
Exited	5	1	6
Not exited, not deradicalized	2	4	6

thus did not know that focal individual's current status (but assumed that they were still radicalized).

Types of Exit and Deradicalization

Below, we discuss stress, disillusionment, and burnout; successful interventions by individuals (or groups of individuals); successful interventions by institutions (including programs and organizations); and self-driven exit from radical extremist organizations or a radical mindset. For the following sections, our *analytic sample* (or denominator) consisted of all focal individuals who had at least exited the radical organization (and, at most, had exited, had deradicalized, and were currently activists)—a total of 26 cases.

Two important caveats apply to the following sections that describe processes involved in exiting radical extremist groups and cognitive or emotional deradicalization. First, these processes (stress, disillusionment, and burnout; successful interventions by individuals; and so on) are not mutually exclusive. Focal individuals can and did experience two or more of these processes. Second, it is important to note that *interventions* by individuals or institutions include both clearly intentional interventions and those that might have been inadvertent or happenstance.

Stress, Disillusionment, and Burnout

Because past research has noted that stress, burnout, and disillusionment are frequently cited reasons for leaving radical organizations, we also coded for this in our sample.[2] Out of 32 focal individuals, 15 (14 white supremacists and one Islamic extremist) indicated that they became disappointed by the hypocrisy or other negative behaviors (such as too much infighting or unproductive levels of violence) in the radical organizations they joined or became exhausted by their own involvement.[3] For example, one former

---

[2]   John Horgan, Mary Beth Altier, Neil Shortland, and Max Taylor, "Walking Away: The Disengagement and De-Radicalization of a Violent Right-Wing Extremist," *Behavioral Sciences of Terrorism and Political Aggression*, Vol. 9, No. 2, May 2017.

[3]   During their time in radical organizations, some individuals described how the stress of involvement in extremism led to suicidal ideation or suicide attempts. One former Islamic extremist explained: "The only reason

white supremacist explained their own experiences of hypocrisy inside the organization: "We're out there marching about illegals bringing drugs into the nation and yet, at the time, I was using illegal drugs. All of these other guys were using illegal drugs. I was partying with some of them, so I saw it personally. So it just started to seem more and more hypocritical and it just didn't make sense to me anymore after a while, after about a year." Another former white supremacist spoke about the exhaustion that constant hate involves: "For me, being involved with that lifestyle became utterly exhausting. Once I found myself out of that lifestyle, I could actually breathe again. My enemy wasn't everywhere. Because when you're in that mindset, when you're in the cult mentality, everybody is the enemy, everybody's the enemy, or a suspect."

Successful Interventions by Individuals

Our respondents described successful interventions by one or more individuals that helped 22 (19 white supremacists and three Islamic extremists) of our 32 focal individuals to exit radical groups, psychologically deradicalize, or remain deradicalized after initial deradicalization.[4] These interventions were often *intentional*, in that they were planned and orchestrated in advance. However, interventions were also sometimes *happenstance*, in that individuals (or organizations, discussed later in this chapter) played an unwitting role in the focal individual's deradicalization. Table 6.2 provides a breakdown of the types of individuals involved in successful interventions, as well as the number of total cases and white supremacist versus Islamic extremist cases in which each type of individual was involved.

Characteristics of Successful Interventions by Individuals

Interventions by the types of individuals listed in Table 6.3 that helped focal individuals deradicalize usually (in all but three cases) provided one or more of the following positive experiences or supports: (1) diverse cultural and demographic exposure, (2) emotional support or kindness, (3) financial stability, and (4) domestic stability. For the three cases in which none of the above positive experiences or support played a role, focal individuals had specific negative experiences that pushed them away from radical movements. These three cases all involved white supremacists; in one case, the focal individual experienced a friend in the radical group dying, which helped push the focal individual away from radicalism. In the other two cases, they experienced betrayal and hypocrisy by other group members, which motivated them to find a way out of the groups.

---

why I didn't kill myself was because my kids. I was just like, oh, I'm still going to go to hell but I was like life is pretty much hell other than my children. And I . . . it was just bad." Also, a former white supremacist described feeling miserable about losing friends to violence, which in turn drove them to two suicide attempts.

[4] The remaining five focal individuals either were deceased or their radicalization status was unknown; see the "Current Status" section.

**Table 6.2
Types of Individuals Involved in Successful Interventions**

Type of Individual Who Intervened	Description	White Supremacist	Islamic Extremist	Total
Diverse acquaintance	Acquaintance who is from a racial or ethnic (or other demographic) group hated by radical ideology of focal individual	11	1	12
Life partner	Husband, wife, boyfriend, girlfriend, or other life partner	6	1	7
Former radical or other professional	Individual who is professionally involved in deradicalization, whether a former radical also or professional antihate activist	6	0	6
Friend	Friend or friends of focal individual	5	1	6
Journalist	Journalist, documentary filmmaker, or other individual involved in media efforts, often who makes the focal individual reconsider their beliefs through thoughtful interviewing	4	0	4
Child	Child or children of focal individual caused change of heart through desire to protect or provide, desire to "break the cycle," etc.	3	1	4
Other family member	Nuclear or extended family of focal individual, whether by blood or marriage (does not include life partners or children of focal individual)	3	1	4
Religious authority	Pastor, imam, religious teacher, etc.	3	1	4
Current radical	Current member of radical organization who convinces focal individual to deradicalize or leave the radical group by exhibiting hypocritical, threatening, or other noxious behavior	3	0	3
Therapist	Therapist providing clinical treatment to focal individual	1	1	2
School official	Teacher, principal, etc.	0	1	1

NOTE: Nineteen focal individuals received successful interventions from more than one type of individual; ten cases involved two types, five cases involved three types, two cases involved four types, and one case involved five types of individuals from this table.

Table 6.3
Characteristics of Successful Interventions by Individuals

Characteristic	Description	White Supremacist	Islamic Extremist	Total
Diverse cultural or demographic exposure	Individual (sometimes multiple individuals in a work or neighborhood context) defies stereotypes, treats focal individual well, or otherwise challenges focal individual's extremist assumptions	14	3	17
Emotional support or kindness	Individual provides (often unexpected) support and kindness to focal individual when they are in difficult circumstances	11	1	12
Financial stability	Individual provides alternate source of income, other financial help, etc. that decreases distress and hopelessness or decreases reliance on the radical organization	3	2	5
Domestic stability	Life partner or other family bonds create stability and incentives to decrease radical activities and affiliations	3	1	4
Noxious or negative impact from radical individuals	Inadvertent "interventions" in which individuals cause experiences that lead a focal individual to want to deradicalize	3	0	3

In the next two sections, we provide additional detail on the two most common features of successful interventions: exposure to diversity and emotional support.

Diverse Cultural and Demographic Exposure

Notably, the most common type of successful interventions by individuals involved these individuals intentionally or inadvertently exposing extremists to cultural or demographic diversity that challenged these extremists' preconceived notions about groups that they hated as part of their ideology. This occurred in 17 cases: 14 white supremacists and three Islamic extremists. For example, one former white supremacist explained: "But I was forced to travel . . . because of the nature of my work. And I found myself in situations where I was faced with things with my perceived enemy . . . and my perceived enemy was treating me normal. . . . It was like I just came from a black neighborhood or I just came from [after working in] a Hispanic neighborhood and all this stuff that you're [other white supremacists are] saying, I didn't see it." Similarly, a former Islamic extremist described how he traveled internationally during his honeymoon, and how "all these different places . . . really impacted me, and it made me become more—it relaxed me a bit."

Sometimes, this exposure to diversity came from specific people in the focal individual's broader social network who challenged their beliefs. For example, one former white supremacist described how such a situation finally disabused him of his radical beliefs:

> A man that I met who was actually in the military with my father—he was a black gentleman and we started talking one day and I asked him, I said, "[name], did you know I was a skinhead for a long time?" And he just looked at me odd and he goes, "A what?" So I told him and he was, like, "Are you serious?" And I said, "Yeah." And he was like, "Well, you've known me since you were a little boy," and I said, "Yeah, I know." And he goes, "You have family that are mixed. So how can you make those claims?" And that was the day I realized that I can't make those claims any more.

Emotional Support or Kindness

The next most common feature of successful interventions (15 cases: 11 white supremacists and four Islamic extremists) was experiencing personal acceptance and emotional support. In some cases, this emotional support came as a surprise—that is, the focal individual was expecting hate or rejection and instead experienced the opposite. For example, one former white supremacist described experiencing emotional support during a church service that helped them deradicalize: "My pastor was doing a service a few months later and he called me up to share my testimony, kind of like a shock. So I got up there and I told the congregation about my past and everything thinking they'd get upset. They all came up and they were shaking my hand and hugging me and everything."

Another former white supremacist described how someone who was working to deradicalize him took him to a café run by former gang members as part of his deradicalization process. While they were eating, he said:

> I remember the girl that waited on us was a black girl and she was like my typical stereotype of what I pictured black gangbanger girls looked like. . . . And I remember she kept staring at me like she wanted something from me, but it was like an angry stare. And I couldn't understand it. And I remember at first, I was really uncomfortable. And I remember [name] was like, "The first step to healing is to acknowledge how you've hurt other people. So I did you a favor, homie. I know that you would not be ready for that step yet so I went ahead and told her who you were. She knows you're KKK, or trying to get out. . . . She's well aware of you. . . . And she's expecting you to come over there and talk to her like a human being."

At first, this individual resisted the process. However, he continued:

I remember, he was not taking no for an answer. He's like, "Go talk to this girl. She's on her break standing there waiting for you to talk to her." And I was like, "Oh my god." I was scared. For the first time, I was scared of what I didn't understand. And I remember I walked up to her and I started to say, "Hi, I'm [name] . . ." And I started to bawl my eyeballs out. Like baby sob. And she grabbed me and she hugged me and she said, "It's okay, man. It feels good to let it out." And I was like, "I am so sorry." And I just started—like, I'm getting emotional right now because that was a really important part of my recovery from hate, and [name] made that happen.

As evidenced by this example, interventions often involved multiple features—in this case, diverse cultural exposure combined with emotional support and (often unexpected) kindness.

Successful Interventions by Institutions

Eleven cases (eight white supremacists and three Islamic extremists) involved interventions by formal, established institutions (including programs and organizations) that played a role in the focal individual deradicalizing or staying deradicalized. These institutions fell into three categories: religious, law enforcement, and secular nonprofit (e.g., 12-step programs, the Museum of Tolerance, Homeboy Industries). Of these 11 cases that received institutional interventions, nine (seven white supremacists and two Islamic extremists) also received interventions from individuals. One of these nine cases (a former white supremacist) received interventions from both religious and nonprofit organizations (as well as interventions from multiple individuals). Clearly, deradicalization was a complex, multistep process for many focal individuals, involving a mix of different individuals and institutions.

Six of these cases involved religious conversion or intervention by religious authorities to help deradicalize focal individuals; five of these were former white supremacists who experienced Christian conversion or acceptance by a congregation as part of their transition from involvement in violent radicalism. One was a former Islamic extremist whose belief in radical Islam was challenged by Sufi teachers. This individual ended up in the Middle East studying with Sufi teachers, who explicitly challenged his more extreme and radicalized beliefs: "So the whole time I was there, you know, it—I just went through a complete cognitive shift, because at the end of every lesson, you know, I'd go back, and I would think about how I viewed certain things, and how I interpreted them." He described what this process of education and self-reflection meant to him: "I went through a proper deradicalization process. I didn't know it at the time. I only learned it later on. But I went through a full cognitive shift. In fact, the sheikh said to me, . . . 'I'm going to give you a new pair of glasses by which to view the world.'"

Three cases (one white supremacist and two Islamic extremists) involved successful interventions involving law enforcement. In the one white supremacist case, threats from law enforcement about a broadening intelligence net helped convince the individual to leave the radical group. This individual explained: "And all of a sudden after the rally, the intelligence service knocked on the door. . . . Yeah. 'We're watching you, just want to let you know. One of your members is doing something; it's your head on the plate.' . . . Then I found out we had a traitor. They infiltrated us. They wiretapped him and recorded everything that happened at the rally. It was bad and I was paranoid." One former Islamic extremist was able to deradicalize after her (more radical) husband was imprisoned and he no longer forbade her to access online materials antithetical to radical Islam. Another former Islamic extremist began to deradicalize while in prison. For the latter case, a family member explained:

> And sitting in isolation by yourself where you have a lot of time to think, a lot of time to recap your whole life, he realized that those people steered him in the wrong place. That they convinced him to do something terrible. He felt bad; he felt horrible about it. He wished that he could turn back the hands of time. . . . So, all you have is time to reevaluate your life and to read the holy Quran 50 times to where you've figured out that the way you was reading it before is the wrong way because now you're seeing it the way it should have been read. So, you're deprogramming yourself and not even knowing you are.

Finally, three cases (all white supremacists) received interventions from various secular nonprofits: 12-step programs, the Museum of Tolerance, Homeboy Industries, and organizations dedicated to deradicalization, such as Parallel Networks and Light upon Light. For example, one former white supremacist explained,

> But it was probably around August or September of last year [2019] that [name] introduced me to the Light upon Light network and Parallel Networks and . . . that was the first time I really saw some bit of light. Because I'm like, holy cow, this is what we need. This is what we need. And then I started getting involved with Light upon Light and Parallel Networks. And that was honestly the first time that I really started kind of dealing with everything I guess you could say. Because I kind of went into kind of shutdown mode after I left [the radical organization] and it was just almost just survival one day after another.

Self-Driven Exit

In addition to experiencing interventions—either by intentional efforts from individuals or organizations or through happenstance occurrences—respondents described how focal individuals sometimes engaged in conscious, self-driven processes of deradicalization. We defined *self-driven exit* as the instance when an individual or their contact described deliberate proactive outreach and the seeking out of philosophical or personal reasons to abandon the radicalized life or organization. Individuals described many different life experiences or changes that led to them questioning their attachment to violent extremism and either gradually or rapidly extracting themselves from radical organizations. Twenty-two out of 35 interviews (involving 20 cases: 18 white supremacists and two Islamic extremists) described processes of self-driven exit from extremism.

For example, one former Islamic extremist respondent described how they spent time away from their extremist partner online, watching TV, reading, or speaking with nonradicals and how this self-driven exploration, motivated by intellectual curiosity, gradually drove them away from extremism. They stated, "I learned from, when I got a TV and I watched PBS and I watched Fox Business. . . . And I really liked the libertarian message and I started learning about the Constitution even though I thought, 'Okay it's not Islamic but this is a really good document and I really like it.'"

A former white supremacist described how he found God and religion after facing a life-threatening health diagnosis, which eventually drove him from extremism:

> And if I'm going to be a practicing Christian, I can no longer be a Nazi because, as the book says, no man can serve two masters. You must love one and turn from the other. So, turning from Nazism might have been a very difficult thing for me to do sometime prior to that, but it certainly wasn't a difficult task for me to do now that I knew that I was going to live. And that just about wrapped that up.

Another former white supremacist described how they began doing research on core messages from the propaganda that helped originally drive them toward extremism. In this case, their curiosity about the causes of racial differences in crime rates helped drive them away from their radical beliefs: "So, I started actually reading, okay, there's all this stuff on black and white crime; what's the truth behind it? What is the stuff in society that makes some of these neighborhoods this way? . . . Like, not only just, well, what makes this community or this group of people this way, but what would it even be like growing up this way? Kind of trying to understand people more."

Failed Interventions

Our interviews revealed that 19 (12 white supremacists and seven Islamic extremists) out of our 32 focal individuals experienced failed interventions by individuals or organizations (or both) at some point in their trajectories of radicalization and deradicalization. Nine of these 19 focal individuals experienced failed interventions by both individuals and organizations.

Of the 15 focal individuals who experienced failed interventions by individuals, the majority of these failed attempts (eight white supremacists and five Islamic extremists) were family members trying to intervene and either having no effect or even increasing the focal individual's dedication to radicalism as a result.[5] For example, one former white supremacist explained:

---

[5]   The remaining two accounts of failed interventions involved friends trying to intervene (one case) and multiple unspecified individuals attempting to intervene (one case).

My grandfather actually pulled me aside to have a talk about being involved in this. And he said, "You know, [name], one of two things is going to happen to you if you continue on this path. They are gonna kill you or imprison you." So this was my grandparent, my grandparents would come to get me out, which I was already 15 years in by this point. And I'll never forget because this was somebody I looked up to ever since I was little. And the horrible thing I said to him was something about like, "I'd rather live my life fighting than on my knees," or something like, "You might have given up but I haven't." And I regret saying that to this day because of the look that I got. But he tried to get me out at that point as well. No effort could get through to me when I was in there because I was so fanatical, so dedicated.

Meanwhile, nine focal individuals (four white supremacists and five Islamic extremists) experienced attempted interventions by organizations that either backfired or had no effect. Most of these attempted interventions (three white supremacists and five Islamic extremists) occurred at the hands of law enforcement or intelligence organizations. For example, the father of one former Islamic extremist explained how his son was caught with a false passport in a foreign country and was put in a political prison: "At that time he was further radicalized by hardcore well-known al Qaeda members in this political jail." Meanwhile, a former white supremacist explained that any police response to their violence against leftist organizations only served to further radicalize them: "What happened is, any time we were pressured, any time the FBI showed up at my house and the cops showed up, or we got in a fight with the ARA [Anti-Racist Action] or Antifa or whatever, or violence was projected against us or anything like that, it further radicalized me." Two former white supremacists (one of whom experienced a failed intervention by law enforcement) also described failed interventions by school officials.

Feeling "Drawn Back" to Radicalism

Prior work describes how ex-radicals who are struggling can feel drawn back to organizations or ideologies.[6] Six of our focal individuals (five white supremacists and one Islamic extremist) described similar feelings.

In some cases, postexit social isolation made focal individuals miss the camaraderie they experienced while part of radical groups. One former white supremacist respondent explained: "When you're in Klan, like, the neighbors that know, even people that may not be offended by it, still don't want that association. So, it's a very isolating kind of a thing, if that makes sense. And that makes it harder to leave as well because then you don't really have any connections in the outside world."

In some cases, feelings of being drawn back were triggered or sustained by current events, as this former right-wing extremist explained:

---

[6]   Simi et al., 2017.

> What it is, is all these statues of Columbus being torn down scares the hell out of me because I'm thinking that people are going to start getting torn down next. . . . How do we cope with that? A lot of the hard-line traditionalists aren't actually all that stubborn; it's just that we're kind of old-fashioned and then society progressed really fast and we kind of got left behind. And we just need a minute to catch up with all this. . . . I am very scared that I'm not really deradicalized, that I'm still going to be kind of racist or sexist or something, and that I'll wind up doing more harm than good. And I'm scared of that.

Similarly, one respondent described how they were actively monitoring current affairs and their own reactions to ongoing news and events, so as to figure out what their safe zone is and when they should not engage with or respond to taunts. As this former right-wing extremist noted:

> And people are asking me, "So are you gonna go defend?" And I did a lot of soul-searching and I can't, man, I can't. This is too close to me. This is way too close to me. This is my religion; this is my race. This seems like it might be worth stabbing people over. It seems like people are going to get hurt if I go down there and try and stop people from tearing down a statue.

Another former white supremacist explained that temptation is always there but peaks with certain political developments:

> To be honest with you, it's kind of always tempting. It's never—maybe a year or two after I got out, I never really—when I was done, to be honest with you, I didn't really think about it any more. It was kind of like, all right, I'm done with that. But yes, as you get older, it is a little bit more tempting to not go to the extreme side. And logically, of course, neo-Nazism is stupid. It doesn't add up. It doesn't make sense. But when you look at what's going on in the world today, yeah sure, it's kind of hard sometimes not to fall back into it.

Conclusion

The respondents in our study described a wide variety of deradicalization journeys. They described factors or circumstances that motivated or accelerated their exits, such as disillusionment with organizational effectiveness, burnout from the frenzy of hate, or successful interventions from individuals or institutions. Notably, they described quite a few failed interventions (especially by institutions, but also some by individuals). The most common feature of successful interventions appeared to be either planned or happenstance exposure to kindness and understanding by members of a group that the individual had come to hate for ideological reasons. In some cases, law enforcement interventions led to successful outcomes, but these interventions seemed equally likely to increase radicalization. More than half of participants also discussed a conscious, self-driven process of deradicalization, set in motion by different life experiences. They also talked about where they are today, indicating that deradicalizing may share features with addiction and sobriety, requiring frequent reinforcement and support to maintain.

CHAPTER SEVEN
Participant Perspectives on Mitigation Strategies

This chapter describes respondents' perspectives on how violent extremism can be mitigated by preventing persons from developing extremist ideologies, preventing them from joining extremist organizations, or deradicalizing those who have joined those organizations. It is important to note that their recommendations are anecdotal and based on their own experiences. Among other reasons, we find it important to include this information in the spirit of *citizen participation*, "the redistribution of power that enables the have-not citizens, presently excluded from the political and economic processes, to be deliberately included in the future."[1] This moves beyond the classic paradigm of researchers making policy recommendations based on the histories and stories of the subjects of their research and engages the individuals who lived these events in the process of making policy and changing practices. Such an approach is still relatively rare in the field of terrorism research.[2] But it is important to keep in mind that we are simply describing recommendations made by those whom we interviewed, neither endorsing nor criticizing these recommendations. We make our own recommendations, partially informed by those made by interviewees, in Chapter Eight.

More importantly, many participants in our research agreed to participate because we took this citizen-involved approach from the outset. One parent of a now-deceased extremist told us: "We have to let the families talk. . . . I said you don't talk for me. Let me talk as a mother or let my son speak as a brother. And so, academics at some point understood." At the conclusion of an interview, another former white supremacist said to us: "I appreciate what you guys are doing because if there's anyone who can tell us about how to combat Nazism in America today, it's former neo-Nazis. And I think that a lot of the methods that people are using to combat white supremacy in the nation they're going about it in a very, very wrong way."

---

[1] S. R. Arnstein, "A Ladder of Citizen Participation," *Journal of the American Institute of Planners*, Vol. 35, No. 4, 1969.

[2] For one exception, see Ryan Scrivens, Vivek Venkatesh, Maxime Bérubé, and Tiana Gaudette, "Combating Violent Extremism: Voices of Former Right-Wing Extremists," *Studies in Conflict and Terrorism*, November 11, 2019.

Analysis of Interviews

We asked open-ended questions of formers and family members for their recommendations on how violent extremism could be prevented. Some opined about efforts that could prevent people from developing extremist ideologies or extremist groups, while others discussed strategies for deradicalizing individuals already part of these groups. We present these recommendations below. In this chapter, we do not provide precise tabulations of how many individuals made specific recommendations, because we were more interested in presenting the breadth of ideas than in how frequently they were endorsed. However, we do convey when recommendations were made by either a single respondent (to indicate interpretive caution) or many respondents (to highlight high-frequency recommendations from our sample).

Respondents' Perspectives on Preventing Radicalization

Perspectives on preventing radicalization focused on conducting interventions during childhood (including education and prosocial activities), exposing individuals to members of different racial and cultural groups, addressing marginalization, addressing polarization and media sensationalism, accessing mental health treatment, and proactively targeting veterans. We discuss the specific recommendations and insights provided by our interviewees in each of these areas.

Intervening During Childhood

As described in Chapter Four, three cases acknowledged some form of trauma that occurred prior to joining an extremist organization, although others might have experienced other forms of trauma that made them more vulnerable to radicalization. Only two of the cases in our sample suggested that addressing issues in the home when they were growing up might have reduced their likelihood of being involved in extremist organizations. For example, a former white supremacist told us: "So, if I could pick a spot for somebody to intervene. . . . [T]he first one would have been during the abusive relationships that my father had with the family. I wish somebody would have come in and . . . removed him from the home." Another former white supremacist grew up in a crowded home and lamented: "It was bad enough that we had bugs, and I didn't want to invite friends over, and it was not a pleasant environment to be in. I didn't have any way to understand that. I had no resources, nobody to help me with that."

More common, however, were recommendations about more-vigilant monitoring of youth by parents and other adults. In some cases, respondents recommended that parents and other adults be trained to look out for *warning signs* (a term specifically used by the father of a boy who joined an Islamic extremist organization), which are not necessarily specific to extremism—such as subtle or dramatic changes in behavior, signs of becoming withdrawn, or new friendship groups. In other cases, respondents advocated that parents watch for even small changes in their children's ideological beliefs. This recommendation is in line with current efforts by the U.S. Department of Homeland Security and various U.S. attorneys who seek to educate audiences on risk factors for extremism and warning signs.[3] One former white supremacist told us: "If someone can be approached before they're fully indoctrinated, in the infant stages of the indoctrination process, I think they can be reached." Two others advocated for such vigilance specifically among school personnel. A friend of a current white supremacist said: "Schools need to do a whole lot more of educating about what causes extremism, how to notice it, how to identify it in their own schools. . . . And it starts in the schools. That's where all the propaganda begins, I'm telling you. For kids, that is where kids start to get the seeds of radicalization and hatred put in their heads." The other, a parent of someone who died after joining ISIS, said: "These are factors that we are trying to mobilize in schools. To be more attentive to a young person who needs attention. And not to discriminate or stigmatize a young person or to get him out of school because we are afraid that he will become a terrorist, no. It is precisely so that he has more attention."[4]

Some interventions that respondents suggested be employed during childhood were more general. For example, one former white supremacist discussed the importance of "tough parenting." Another former white supremacist stated: "I think just when I was young [it would have helped to have] people around that were steering me in the right direction rather than me raising myself." Similarly, a family member of an Islamic extremist discussed the importance of mentors, especially male role models, because "most of the youth, the father's not at home." A former white supremacist was haunted by their digital footprint made while participating in extremist organizations and advocated for "a commercial which says, 'what you say online stays forever,'" because "if you could show maybe a normal kid in high school and him going on the computer saying crazy stuff and then maybe five or ten years later he can't find a job and he's homeless or something like that. You know, like, some kind of shock value just like the anticigarette ads do where what you say and do on the internet lasts forever."

Education for Youth

Eight respondents (one former Islamic extremist, the family member of an Islamic extremist, and six former white supremacists) stressed the importance of education, and those who mentioned education also mentioned its importance, emphatically. Such comments included "education is key"; "education is also a key thing"; "education would have to do with a lot of it"; "we have to start in schools"; "education really needs to be a huge, huge piece"; and "that [education] would be the first thing; that would be my hugest focus."

---

[3] See the description of community awareness briefing and community resilience exercises in Jackson et al., 2019b.

[4] Friends can also play a critical role in helping to detect and intervene in the radicalization process. See Williams, Horgan, and Evans, 2016.

Within the topic of education, two themes emerged. Most often, respondents stressed the importance of education that exposes students to other cultures, religions, and religious history, which, in at least one case, might have been effective at countering what the former white supremacist heard "growing up in [their] own house": "That really had a very negative impact on my way of thinking." A separate theme stressed that schools "have to change that whole mindset" and include education on compassion, sensitivity training, critical thinking, and meditation, specific terms referenced by two former white supremacists and the parent of an Islamic extremist. One activist former white supremacist described a program his organization runs that integrates these themes:[5]

> It's arts driven, service learning and global engagement. So we ask students what they're concerned about in society. They tell us and then we facilitate ways to address those issues. We got [a] solution-driven way . . . and they do it with connection and guidance of a really amazing roster of people called global mentors, which are from all over the world, formers and survivors, to inspire our students with their stories but also like advise them and give them guidance on their service learning projects, and it's really about weaving social fabric and developing a healthy sense of identity, purpose, and belonging, which having an unhealthy sense of is at-risk factor for violent extremism.

However, at least two former white supremacists criticized the way they were taught, saying that it contributed to the development of their ideology. As one articulated: "We were taught growing up, things that are sort of up for debate," and that "if I could have had some of those things presented in a more factual manner by a professional rather than a propagandist, that could have made more sense to me. . . . [I]f I could have had something that felt a little more like it lined up a little more with reality that I observed in my life but it was coming from a professional, like a better source, that could have kept me from going off the deep end." He told us that these circumstances contributed directly to his conversion to extremism: "it was like the only place that I could get another perspective on it was like the NSM and that type of far-right propaganda." Another former white supremacist said:

> We really need to have some kind of resource there that addresses the politically incorrect questions that people like me had. You know, I had questioned like, "Why is it that we have, that we're making a big fuss about Chinese New Year when we don't make a fuss over, you know, holidays that, so-called Euro-Canadians celebrate?" Why are we emphasizing these things? Why are these people that are new to my school, why don't they seem more interested in communicating in English? . . . It's not acceptable to me that the only resource that I had, that I could feel safe

---

[5]   See Chapter Six for a formal definition of *activist* on the deradicalization spectrum.

in asking the questions and get any kind of answer at all was, you know, leaders of [country's] largest hate group.

Providing Activities for Youth

Beyond education, at least three respondents mentioned the need for prosocial activities for youth.[6] A former white supremacist told us: "I was very young when I got in, when I joined. And not being able to really join anything else like that is another reason why I went in." Another former white supremacist provided a general recommendation: "We need to give kids as many options as possible to make the world a better place in an actual productive way that makes the world better." This individual, in fact, recalled: "[F]or me, joining racist extremists was the answer for me at that point in time. I really felt, and I'm sure for you it sounds crazy, but I felt that by spreading hate I was making the world a better place." Another former white supremacist recalled taking a martial arts class as a youth but that his family could not afford to continue his classes: "So now I'm really pissed off because I can't stay in judo . . . but I think if I would have been able to stay in judo that would have made a huge difference in my path."

Exposure to Different Races and Cultures

Respondents were not solely focused on exposing school students to different races, cultures, and religions; at least eight respondents recommended greater exposure across society to members of different groups. Two former white supremacists told us that such exposures would have prevented them from radicalizing. One said, "If I had more contact with black people, with Jewish people, with people of color in general at that point in time, at that juncture [after he had been a crime victim], it would have been a very different thing." The other stated: "If I had a best friend who was black, there was no way I was—I can't say I was a neo-Nazi. That just doesn't work." A friend of a white supremacist said, similarly: "Him having an actual conversation with somebody who didn't look like him, someone other than his white friends telling him that he was wrong. He was only getting negative feedback. He never sat down with a person of color and had a conversation about anything."

Some respondents also offered formal structures for promoting such integration or exposure. For example, one former white supremacist marveled at the power of the internet for providing exposure to diversity: "We can travel anywhere on the face of this earth virtually through our phone, through our desktop, our laptop, our iPad. And begin learning about different cultures and different people." The family member

---

[6]   Although the impact of such activities is unclear on mitigating the risk for extremism, various CVE programming has undertaken this approach. The goal of these programs is to use activities, such as extracurricular sports and other activities, as a means to provide youth access to adult mentorship and provide opportunities for socialization. See, for example, Amelia Johns, Michele Grossman, and Kevin McDonald, "'More Than a Game': The Impact of Sport-Based Youth Mentoring Schemes on Developing Resilience Toward Violent Extremism," *Social Inclusion*, Vol. 2, No. 2, 2014.

of a now-deceased Islamic extremist described a program that the family member created, a cultural "exchange program" for university students studying to become teachers, that included lectures on his country of origin's culture and history, opportunities to shadow teachers in the neighborhoods with large population from that country, and field trips to local mosques. However, a few people criticized some of the formal programs they had been exposed to; for example, one former white supremacist reflected on sensitivity videos shown in workplaces as "insulting and detached."

It should be noted that similar efforts have been undertaken to promote interfaith dialogues and gatherings. In efforts to counter Islamic extremism, for example, efforts would bring members of local mosques, churches, and synagogues together to build interfaith relationships, bridge a common divide, and reduce the risk of stereotypes so easily developed against those who are different.[7] Similar kinds of cross-cultural exposure may also hold promise for countering extremism. We discuss such strategies in more detail in Chapter Eight.

Addressing Marginalization

Another recommendation that emerged across respondents was more systemic—that extremism is born from people's actual or perceived marginalization. Such concerns resonate with literature articulating the need to offer opportunities for expressing grievances.[8] In comments resonating with sentiments expressed earlier in this chapter, some respondents who were former white supremacists claimed that there was no avenue to express (in their words) "legitimate" beliefs except within extremist organizations. For example, they stated,

> There is no space for working-class people that have legitimate critiques of globalism, the impact of immigration on low-income workers, cultural issues, . . . so if they want to engage in political white nationalism, the best they can hope for is losing their jobs if they get found out, getting beaten up by antifascists; or if they win a fight against the antifascists, getting arrested for defending themselves. . . . If you feel under attack and you've tried every step of the way to engage in the political process or you've watched other people do that and there's no other way, why wouldn't you turn to violence?

Another former white supremacist offered a similar perspective:

> [B]ecause if you just show up and say, "Hey, I feel like these affirmative action laws are unfair because it doesn't include white people," well, then you're a racist. And it's just this conversation-stopper where you either have to just shut up and back

---

[7] Todd C. Helmus, Erin York, and Peter Chalk, *Promoting Online Voices for Countering Violent Extremism*, Santa Monica, Calif.: RAND Corporation, RR-130-OSD, 2013.

[8] Paul K. Davis and Kim Cragin, eds., *Social Science for Counterterrorism: Putting the Pieces Together*, Santa Monica, Calif.: RAND Corporation, MG-849-OSD, 2009.

down and accept you can't be comfortable in your own skin here, or you double down and say, "My skin is my uniform now and I'm gonna go hang out with the skinheads." And I would like there to be a middle ground where there could be some sort of negotiation.

A few interviewees were also aggrieved that media portrayals of the white working class tended to "dehumanize" them and present them as "backwoods morons that have no legitimate grievances about globalism, capitalism, the impact of imperialism, access to health care, education, all these things." The parent of a former white supremacist also discussed that the labels cast on groups with certain beliefs were alienating: "And I think empowering not just white people but all people to feel that their voices are heard, and trying to work collectively on suggestions instead of forcibly silencing them and dehumanizing them through calling them like scum and whatnot, and evil, evil Nazis just because you want to maybe restrict immigration or whatever, that that's the way to handle it."

Proposed solutions to these issues varied from changing political discourse to providing spaces to express one's grievances. For example, a parent of a deceased Islamic extremist stated, "[M]inorities must continue to be represented at the political level so that we can discuss and avoid scenarios such as departures to Syria that have been a global phenomenon." This was shared by a former white supremacist who discussed marginalization caused by "alienation from the political system": "Everyone is cut off from one another where you don't know your neighbors, you're not involved in civic institutions, all the things that lead to good mental health and community engagement that we know is necessary for a successful community." This individual now works for an organization that aims "to reduce violence but also find ways to address systemic problems in society and humanize individuals as a way to reduce violence."

Others expressed frustration over other systemic issues that disproportionately affect marginalized populations or that keep them marginalized, such as unemployment. Proposed solutions, which are in keeping with the established relationship between unemployment and right-wing extremism,[9] emphasized addressing the root of these disparities. The former white supremacist who criticized the media's portrayal of white working-class individuals quoted above also stated: "I don't think we can address any of these issues without addressing economic inequality, health care, mental health care, the breakdown of the family, drug addiction, and just the broken souls of these people. Like what do they have to live for? They have nothing to lose between poverty, broken families, broken communities, decaying infrastructure." One activist in our study who was not a former but works to deradicalize extremists tied the disappearance of coal-mining jobs to recruitment in white supremacist organizations. According to

---

[9] See, for example, Armin Falk, Andreas Kuhn, and Josef Zweimüller, "Unemployment and Right-Wing Extremist Crime," *Scandinavian Journal of Economics*, Vol. 113, No. 2, 2011.

him, white coal miners are laid off in place of less expensive migrant workers, leaving the white coal miners

> not employable. The bank is knocking on the door because they haven't been paying their mortgage or their rent so they're going to foreclose on their property and all this kind of thing. So they're out of work, they don't know what to do. The Klan will come into a town like that and hold a rally and say, "Now look, the blacks have the NAACP [National Association for the Advancement of Colored People], you could choose to have the ADL [Anti-Defamation League], nobody stands up for the white man but the Ku Klux Klan. Your job isn't gone, but some [racist term] or some [racist term] has got your job. You've worked there for years and years. Your family's worked there for years and years. Why does that person have your job and you're sitting here? You can't put food on your family's table. You can't put clothes on your child's back. You come join us. Come join the Ku Klux Klan; we'll get your job back."

Addressing Polarization and Media Sensationalism

Many of the participants also spoke of the increasing polarization of American society and media sensationalism; however, they did not necessarily offer specific recommendations for addressing these larger issues. For example, one former white supremacist said: "I think the biggest thing is like everybody is so busy pointing the fingers that they won't stop and listen to people." Another specifically referenced the media's coverage of Dylann Roof, who perpetrated the Charleston church shooting in 2015. This respondent, the spouse of a former white supremacist, said: "The media puts these things out there. Like Dylann Roof; Dylann Roof was part of an organization, okay? Guess what happens? They praise this kid. They say, 'Oh, he was in this group or this group or this group.' And guess what the younger community sees: 'Oh, I want to do that. This is what he does. I want to do that.'"

Mental Health Treatment

Although mental health treatment was discussed extensively as a strategy for deradicalization (see the "Respondents' Perspectives on Promoting Deradicalization" section in this chapter), it was specifically mentioned by only two respondents as an important intervention for preventing radicalization. "[I]f I could have been on the medication then that I'm now [Adderall], that would have helped, and if I would have had better skills at developing a social life or a social circle," said one former white supremacist. Also, the father of a former white supremacist said: "If they see a change in their sons' or daughters' perception, view, language, music, their group of friends, all that stuff, seek some help . . . you've got to be able to talk to health professionals. And health professionals have to be a little bit more attuned to what's going on in society, not just their little circle of professional expertise." However, the family member of a now-deceased Islamic extremist indicated that such resources are not accessible for many:

"The cost for a psychologist or counselor, you're looking $200–$300 an hour. Who can afford that?" This individual also mentioned being dissatisfied with the type of mental health care their son received: "Even watching this with my younger son, what we've gone through with mental health here with him and his depression, it's downright scary. They're completely incompetent to the point where they can cause much more damage."

Outreach to Veterans

Two individuals stated that veterans leaving the military should receive specific outreach for preventing radicalization. Two perspectives were offered. One, a veteran himself and former white supremacist, said: "We go through such a long process of radicalizing our soldiers—and I'm just going to call it what it is. We radicalize troops to send them over there to indiscriminately kill, maim, and destroy whatever it is that files an opposing force to us and our 13 minerals and oil." He recommended "a program to deradicalize U.S. soldiers when they come back from hostile combat." The other signaled that economic forces make veterans uniquely prone to joining extremist groups, aligning with the sentiments expressed on marginalization above. This former white supremacist said,

> I think veterans are particularly prone to it. Like they get out of the military, you get up and go to work every single day, you have a steady paycheck as long as you're not getting yourself in trouble or whatever. So when you're like, hey, how am I going to pay my bills and you get mad, upset, and then start drinking beer or whatever and watch something stupid on TV and, hey, that sounds like a good idea.

Indeed, with the discovery that veterans played a significant role in the mob attack against the U.S. Capitol, the need to help limit the risk of radicalization among military and veteran populations is a growing concern.[10]

Respondents' Perspectives on Promoting Deradicalization

Respondents also provided recommendations to facilitate deradicalization. In particular, they spoke of the need to reach extremists at the right time and place and provided recommendations on who delivers the message (e.g., former extremists), social support from former extremists, and the way to engage extremists. Respondents also discussed the importance of unplanned exposures to diversity and kindness in a person's deradicalization journey, religious education, criticisms of the criminal justice system's approach to radicalized individuals, mental health interventions, and the need for support of families of extremists. We discuss each of these themes below.

---

[10] See, for example, Peter W. Singer and Eric B. Johnson, "The Need to Inoculate Military Servicemembers Against Information Threats: The Case for Digital Literacy Training for the Force," *War on the Rocks*, February 1, 2021.

Right Time, Right Place

As described in Chapter Six, deradicalization is a process that is often facilitated by external individuals or organizations seeking to deradicalize an individual. Many interviewees told us that such messages have to come "at the right time," when "they're ready to hear the message." Another former white supremacist likened the process of deradicalization to that of those with substance use disorders achieving sobriety: "It almost has to be done organically, similar to 12-step programs. Nobody is going to leave until they're ready."

Former-Extremist Spokespersons

Many respondents indicated that messages from those who had been part of extremist organizations and who had deradicalized were important for deradicalization efforts. In fact, the family member of an Islamic extremist who was in prison told us that the family member was trying to convince the extremist to do such outreach from prison: "We want to help him understand, help him educate himself through the prison cells on how he can reach out beyond those cells and help other young men and women to not take the path he took."[11]

However, at least one former white supremacist told us that such outreach can come at a cost. This individual was in a documentary in which they identified as a neo-Nazi, although they had since deradicalized. They were invited to discuss the film at a local university and recounted:

> everyone was so angry and livid. When I look back on that environment of that day like it was just, everyone was so close to losing their cool on me. It was really super stressful and I was feeling so confused and remorseful. I was really very upset that I had hurt people like that. . . . It was also the start of my new life's work actually of educating about racist extremism and the danger of hate groups that I'm still doing now. It's something that I've also struggled with. Like, do I really want to even have any part of my life that's involved at all with this stuff? Like I could just walk away and I could just never talk about it again. That is an option, and I don't think anybody would blame me if I took it.

In fact, former extremists have played a critical role in helping to counter violent extremism. In 2010, Google's think-do tank, Google Ideas (now named Jigsaw), helped create a network of former violent extremists that sought to help counter violent extremism and promote extremist disengagement.[12] Since then, the role of formers has increased,

---

[11] Such intervention efforts have been attempted online in a study that enlisted former extremists to reach out to current extremists via Facebook Messenger. See Frenett and Dow, 2014.

[12] For more on the role of the then-named Google Ideas on developing the counterextremism network, see Helmus, York, and Chalk, 2013.

with one organization, Life After Hate, recently receiving significant funding from the Department of Homeland Security.[13]

Ongoing Support from Former Extremists

Many of our respondents stated that individuals trying to leave extremist organizations need help or support from other former extremists when leaving their organizations. The father of a former white supremacist told us: "[E]verybody needs help to get out. I don't care who you are, you can't do it yourself. . . . And I'm talking about support from other guys and some gals that he knew that had gotten out of organizations." The need for support was attributed to many things; for example, the activist who works to deradicalize individuals stated: "They're joiners to begin with, that's why they went and joined one of these organizations. So if you don't provide that anchor, that support, and they're out there swinging in the wind, like I said, we all want to be loved." Another former white supremacist suggested that the need for support will be long term: "There will always be challenges. There will be a need for, you know, support. There's a need out there for people who've been out for a long time to still have, you know, people that they can check in with. Friends and family that will support them." Because formers' support networks may be weak, this same respondent stated that, "in absence of those kind of connections, they need to have some kind of organization that will provide, you know, some kind of ongoing support, whether it's like in a monthly online support group or whatever is considered useful." Without support, the activist who works to deradicalize individuals warned, "they will seek it elsewhere. So since they can't go back to the organization they just left, they will seek out something else. It may be alcohol, it may be drugs. It may be some other cult."

This support was deemed so critical because many of the formers discussed the psychological and social difficulties individuals face upon leaving these organizations. The father of a former white supremacist explained: "[I]t's somebody to talk to . . . those individuals are so alone now. They don't have friends any more because the only friends they had were their comrades or whatever they call them in that cult." A former white supremacist told us, "I kind of went into kind of shutdown mode after I left, and it was just almost just survival one day after another." They went on to warn:

> [S]o when people leave and there's no one or nothing around, typically one of two things happen. Either they become very self-isolated, very depressed, and they just kind of keep moving on with life but it's very lonely . . . or they come out, they deal with the isolation and they deal with depression, they realize that this society that begged for them to leave this hate and everything else refuses to accept them

---

[13] The organization Life After Hate, which was started by a former right-wing extremist, received a $750,000 grant from Department of Homeland Security. Deepa Bharath, "Organization of Former Extremists Gets $750,000 from DHS to Counter Threats from the Far Right," *Orange County Register*, October 4, 2020.

because of what they were involved in before, so then they get more angry and they go right back.

Nonconfrontational Approach

There was consistency in how respondents described approaching and attempting to deradicalize members of extremist groups. They stressed the importance of listening and being nonconfrontational. One activist who deradicalizes individuals told us:

> [T]hey're not used to sitting around with your enemy and the person actually listening to them. So when I listen to them, that wall begins to come down. . . . I have allowed them to be heard. And so now they feel the need to reciprocate. But now, when it's my turn to be heard by them and their wall is down, I do not attack them. I don't say, "You're wrong. You did this and the Klan did that," and blah-blah-blah. I don't attack them. I simply defend myself.

Another former white supremacist explained: "[N]ot in a confrontational manner because that doesn't work, screaming at somebody or telling them they're wrong, or even being argumentative." Although most people indicated that these messages should come from trusted allies, one former Islamic extremist did suggest that the U.S. Department of State track radical plans on social media and respond online with open-ended questions, such as: "How do you think this benefits your religion?" "How do you think this shows a good image of the prophet?" Indeed, this nonconfrontational approach has received scientific support in the literature on conspiracy theories, with public health experts encouraging nonconfrontational engagement with conspiracy theorists.[14]

Positive Exposure to Different Races and Cultures

As with efforts to prevent radicalization, a few individuals discussed the importance of exposures to people of different races or cultures as important for deradicalization. A former white supremacist told us: "I believe that one of the best ways to deal with people during their disengagement is to expose them to the perceived enemy and to see that the perceived enemy is just another human being just like them; has a lot of the same struggles just like them. They bleed red. They have kids, they have families. They have needs just like everybody else." However, as mentioned above, some extremists

---

[14] William Marcellino, Todd C. Helmus, Joshua Kerrigan, Hilary Reininger, Rouslan I. Karimov, and Rebecca Ann Lawrence, *Detecting Conspiracy Theories on Social Media: Improving Machine Learning to Detect and Understand Conspiracy Theories*, Santa Monica, Calif.: RAND Corporation, RR-A676-1, forthcoming. For original sources, see, for example, Fabiana Zollo, Petra Kralj Novak, Michela Del Vicario, Alessandro Bessi, Igor Mozetič, Antonio Scala, Guido Caldarelli, and Walter Quattrociocchi, "Emotional Dynamics in the Age of Misinformation," *PLoS ONE*, Vol. 10, No. 9, September 2015; Maryke S. Steffens, Adam G. Dunn, Julie Leask, and Kerrie E. Wiley, "How Organisations Promoting Vaccination Respond to Misinformation on Social Media: A Qualitative Investigation," *BMC Public Health*, Vol. 19, No. 1, 2019.

are not always receptive to such messages. One former white supremacist told us, "If they would have sat me down with a Holocaust survivor, I would have listened, I would have been polite, and would have let that build into being a neo-Nazi."

When discussing recommendations for promoting deradicalization, two former white supremacists highlighted stories of unplanned exposures that were instrumental in their deradicalization process.[15] In one, a respondent had left one organization to form his own and was looking for a new home for himself and his family. A Turkish Muslim "was the only one who'd rent to us. And it was the relationship with him that shaped it, that made me not form that other Klan group. . . . It was the compassion there that he showed to me, that broke the last 20 percent of hate I had." In the other instance, a black cashier at a store noticed the respondent's tattoo that reflected an extremist ideology and said:

> "I know that's not who you are and you're a better person than that," and I just grabbed my food and ran out of there, and I went home and I got drunk as I could as fast as I could, and I went out and attacked someone on the street trying to put distance between myself and this moment of kindness I experienced, and that was like within the first few months of my involvement. So it took seven years for that act of kindness to really come to fruition, but what it ultimately did it was as much of a factor in me leaving as anything else, and that's why I think kindness is such an important asset.

There is an extensive body of research, stemming from Allport's "contact hypothesis," originally published in 1954,[16] that examines whether intergroup contact, as recommended by some respondents, reduces prejudice. Although reviewing that literature was beyond the scope of our study, one comprehensive review found that "cross-group contact is an essential, if insufficient, component for lasting remedies."[17] However, that review also stressed that cross-group *friendships* are especially important for achieving desired effects.

Religious Education

Across both white supremacists and Islamic extremists, many recommended the importance of religious education. In some instances, respondents thought that adopting religious ideologies and practices was part of the deradicalization process. Both Christianity and Buddhism were mentioned specifically. The wife of a former white supremacist told us: "What they need to do is pick up a Bible and start reading and go to church and leave that stuff behind." A former white supremacist said: "Buddhism

---

[15] Such interventions are described more broadly in Chapter Six.

[16] Gordon W. Allport, *The Nature of Prejudice*, Reading, Mass.: Addison-Wesley, 1979.

[17] Thomas F. Pettigrew, Linda R. Tropp, Ulrich Wagner, and Oliver Christ, "Recent Advances in Intergroup Contact Theory," *International Journal of Intercultural Relations*, Vol. 35, 2011.

. . . [is] one of the things that I did deliberately because I was worried that I wasn't really deradicalized. And I did notice I was still holding some hate in my heart and holding a grudge and being a little dismissive of certain people. So I got into yoga." In other cases, and specifically among Islamic extremists, religious education was a way to relearn the tenets of their faith. One former Islamic extremist said that they took a course in Sufism: "So, that really opened my eyes to, you know, to Sufism. I went through a proper deradicalization process."

Criticism of Legal Interventions and Recommendations for Improvement

Four recommendations were brought up regarding how the criminal justice system responds to extremism. First, respondents asked to make sure that law enforcement provide not just a punitive approach but also opportunities for "softer" interventions. According to the parent of an Islamic extremist, fear of a strong-armed police force affects "women who their kids are missing but they're afraid to report to law enforcement." They continued: "I hear a lot in the community, they're afraid to call the police, their kids are missing. The boys are missing. They don't know where their boys are." A family member who reported a former white supremacist to authorities (before they were deradicalized) described how they grappled with the issue: "Don't be afraid. Don't get me wrong. I was terrified. I felt like I was stepping on my [family member's] toes, but you have to be that bigger person to where it's like they're not loving theirself right now. They're not happy with theirself. They need you to be that person to help them."

This tension between an individual's need for interventions and support that can steer them out of extremism and law enforcement's tendency to prioritize criminal investigations is addressed in a recent RAND assessment of U.S. government terrorism-prevention efforts.[18]

At least two recommendations were made for addressing distrust with local law enforcement. The family member of a now-deceased Islamic extremist described his community's enforcement agency's effort to recruit more police officers who were representative of the community, and the father of a different deceased Islamic extremist spoke of workshops he now delivers to "teach [police] how to better work with families." In addition, two family members of an Islamic extremist currently in prison wished that law enforcement had told them that their family member was under surveillance. The family believes that they would not have let him move out of the home, which they felt was instrumental in his carrying out a violent attack, if they had known that he was under investigation or if they had known "what the embassy found out and what the State Department found out and what the FBI agents who interrogated him found out."

Second, respondents argued that, in some cases, prisons and jails can exacerbate extremist ideologies or facilitate involvement in extremist groups. In one instance, a

---

[18] Jackson et al., 2019b.

former Islamic extremist suggested: "When a young person gets caught up in something . . . there should be some kind of mentoring, or peer group that is tasked to stay with the person through their court experience. Because that can accelerate the radicalization process. That is actually the first point of entry." In two other instances, the individual's stature was elevated in prison—in one case, by other prisoners: "He was in a Muslim gang. He was their sheikh and he taught them about the religion. He was the only one who spoke Arabic. . . . [T]hey all looked up to him and, you know, it all inflated his ego because he felt like he was important." And in another, simply going to jail was symbolic. A former white supremacist recounted: "When I got out, I got right back involved. Because I was a victim, I was a victim. I'm a white man. They put me in jail because I'm a white man fighting for the white race. I'm a political prisoner." This was echoed by another white supremacist who said: "I would do away with gang units.[19] I understand the concept but the execution is not helping. Every time one of these states put somebody in a gang unit, they're viewed as a hero."

Third, there was criticism about the prison environment and the lack of programming. A parent of an Islamic extremist in Europe described daily life:

> They have an hour of freedom a day. They can get out of their cell three times, 20 minutes each: 20 minutes in the morning for breakfast, 20 minutes in the afternoon, 20 minutes in the evening, and all day there is no television. They can't read. There are no books. They get Xanax, medication, painkillers. So, chemically, they are doing their job, a chemical straitjacket. They're giving them medicine. But intellectually, there is nothing that is changing.

According to the family member of an Islamic extremist currently in prison: "Just imagine if he got the help in the prison to deprogram himself and to get someone to mentor him, to make him better, someone to help him to be able to help other people. Just imagine where he would be right now and the state of mind he would be right now if he had that." Specifically, the family member suggested programs in which the extremist, and other prisoners, is "able to educate and do research so that he can have the resources to help somebody else. . . . Put someone in place that he can talk to, that he can still give thoughts out to. . . . Put someone in place based off of his religion that he can talk to." However, a former white supremacist who is now an activist and works to help people deradicalize indicated: "Getting in touch with guys in prison isn't as easy because a lot of prisons now, you have to be authorized to write to them. . . . So, it's a little harder reaching out one-on-one to guys in prison."

Fourth, respondents recommended that education be compulsory for prison and jail inmates. The wife of an Islamic extremist told us, "[W]ell for prison I would make mandatory online education for all prisoners because I know that a lot of people just

---

[19] In using the term *gang unit*, the respondent was referring to restrictive or segregated housing in prisons assorted by likely membership in gangs, which also can result in racial segregation.

waste their time in there sleeping." A former white supremacist said, "I would have these gang members and supremacist members from both sides sit down in the same room and, number one, start with education, start teaching them again."

Finally, the family member of a former Islamic extremist mentioned the importance of restorative justice:[20]

> When you're on a quest for forgiveness, whether it's the victims or the perpetrators . . . it's a job that is done [over a] long time. But for that you have to have spaces for discussion and exchange. You have to talk, you have to see people. But if we punish them like dogs, all the time in a corner. Strangled with a leash where you can exceed just about 20 centimeters. The day they let you go, you're going to run as far as you can and you're going to explode.

Mental Health Interventions

As described in an earlier section, formers discussed the process of deradicalizing as both a very lonely and isolating experience. Some spoke of either formal or informal mental health interventions to help them navigate the experience.

Two respondents stated explicitly that they or their family members benefited from formal mental health treatment. A former white supremacist said, "I do think that in college when I tried to go back again, it was nice having student mental health services to talk to." When a parent told us their son now sees a therapist, we asked whether it helps: "A lot. A lot," they replied. A parent of an Islamic extremist suggested that "instead of giving jail time, very long time, I think they need [to] help the young generation. I think they need to build some sort of resource that they can have therapists and mental health evaluation [and] counseling."

However, some lamented that formal mental health care was also inaccessible. The former white supremacist who above told us that he benefited from student mental health services followed up his response by saying: "[O]ne of the reasons that I haven't seen a psychiatrist lately is because I just can't afford it. I totally think I would benefit from it, but it's inaccessible." A few others also mentioned the lack of resources for persons deradicalizing who need mental health support. Some emphasized the lack of support for nonprofit organizations working in this area; a former white supremacist told us: "Yes, we have some nonprofit organizations here in the United States; however, because of the financing of these sorts of groups . . . every fiscal year [there are] some people going, 'Oh, no, where's our money, where's our money, are we gonna get our money?'" There were also criticisms specifically of an inadequate mental health system. According to one former white supremacist: "Mental health is horrible. People

---

[20] Restorative justice is a theory of criminal justice that "emphasizes repairing the harm caused by criminal behavior." See Centre for Justice Reconciliation, "Lesson 1: What Is Restorative Justice?" webpage, undated.

are being dumped out on the street with untreated whatever—untreated alcoholism, untreated mental health issues. And so it's a systemic issue."

Perhaps due to inaccessible formal mental health care, some respondents spoke of informal mental health care that they sought out themselves.[21] According to a former white supremacist: "I do a lot of meditating, which, for me, the introspection and the self-awareness that is brought about from that has been imperative in my mental health. I do still have some mental health issues . . . but I'm very aware of them and I do work on them on a regular basis." Another former white supremacist sought informal care through his own study. He told us: "I've worked very, very hard over the years; different kinds of mental health-type stuff. I've studied a lot of philosophy and psychology on my own. I've spent hours and hours reading and listening to podcasts and different things that kind of helped me reconstruct the way that I view the world and the way that I view suffering."

Support for Families

For this study, RAND collaborated with an organization, Parents For Peace, known for its outreach efforts to and support for the friends and families of those suffering from extremist ideologies. Hence, it is not surprising that some respondents stressed the need for support for families and friends. One family member of a former Islamic extremist said, "I love my community, but sometimes I don't like what they do." She also mentioned that, after her son was arrested, "instead of helping, they bully [her] a lot." Another parent of a now-deceased Islamic extremist told us: "We just didn't want other families to have to deal with that hurt and that pain that we dealt with, that we're still dealing with. Parents for Peace kind of helps us talk about it. The more and more we talk about it, the more it doesn't hurt as bad." Another parent told us about taking to the internet to find other mothers like herself. She found one, and went to visit her, saying:

> I connected with her and that's when I recognized the power of that human connection to be able to relate to somebody who really understood what you were feeling without bad judgment because they were there. They knew, they had the same thing happen to them. How could they judge me, right? And so it created that strength. And it helped lift me up and give me the strength each day and I can feel comfortable sharing memories. And you need to do that, it's part of the healing process. I felt like I finally had the support that I needed.

---

[21] This type of self-driven exit from radicalization is also discussed in Chapter Six.

Conclusion

The respondents in our study provided valuable recommendations on what they believed would be most effective for mitigating extremism. They provided recommendations on how to prevent radicalization, as well as how to deradicalize individuals who were in organizations. Recommendations ranged from addressing systemic issues, such as marginalization and unemployment, to very specific suggestions about who should deliver deradicalization messages, when, and in what way. That said, one should keep in mind our recruitment strategy: The recommendations provided by our respondents likely reflect those promoted by such organizations as Parents for Peace and Beyond Barriers. Other family members, friends, and former extremists who are not formally part of organizations like these, or who attribute deradicalization to other forces, may provide an entirely unique set of recommendations.

These recommendations should not be viewed as based on formal scientific evidence, but it is important to consider them from a citizen science perspective. More importantly, in a field with very few evidence-based interventions for preventing violent extremism (or promoting deradicalization), the insights from the group of those who have been through the process or touched by it should be given serious consideration. In the next chapter, we conclude this report and make our own recommendations based on the results of all of our analysis, the extant literature, and a nod to the recommendations made by the study participants.

CHAPTER EIGHT

Synthesis and Recommendations

Strengths and Limitations

This study privileges the accounts of 32 white supremacists and Islamic extremists, drawing on interviews with formers themselves, as well as their family members and other social relationships. As evidenced by the dearth of firsthand accounts in the existing literature, such data are hard to come by. We believe that these narrative accounts are well worth the effort to obtain and analyze. As observed in this study, narratives from formers and family members both (1) throw descriptive and explanatory light on how factors that are often treated as quantitative variables have complex, time-dependent, and often counterintuitive effects on individuals' radicalization and deradicalization and (2) reveal novel causal processes and dynamics that may be missed by secondary-data analysis or survey-based data collection.

Of course, our approach also has several limitations. Relying on convenience sampling through existing activist organizations seeking to counter extremism brings inherent bias to our sample; quite simply, we spoke with and about individuals who were both (1) far enough "on the other side" of radicalization and its consequences (through deradicalization, imprisonment, or the violent death of the focal individual) and (2) motivated to help others avoid radicalization or deradicalize to a sufficient extent that they wanted to speak with us. Thus, by design, our study did not include cases in which focal individuals were still actively involved in radical activities or organizations.

Our interview approach was also loosely structured, to allow formers and their family members to focus on parts of the radicalization and deradicalization processes that they felt were most important. As a result, we did not systematically ask each respondent about the importance of mental health, substance use, financial struggles, religion, or any other topic; rather, we let respondents tell the story, mentioning factors and processes that they felt were most important along the way. Therefore, we do not have systematic quantitative data on the prevalence of various *candidate mechanisms* for radicalization or deradicalization.

Main Findings

Our sample was highly heterogeneous, covering cases of radicalization occurring across multiple decades, in multiple geographic regions, and with a wide variety of groups and ideologies. Moreover, we interviewed a mix of focal individuals, family members, and other social contacts of former white supremacists and Islamic extremists. Although challenging for analysis, this heterogeneity was also in some ways a strength; covering such a wide variety of circumstances and viewpoints, we discovered many common features of radicalization and deradicalization shared across time, community, age, demographics, and life circumstances and experiences:

1. Abuse or trauma, difficult family life, economic struggles, bullying and discrimination, and other negative life events can lead to distress,[1] as well as delinquency and mental health struggles. These life events and their psychological and behavioral consequences are sometimes implicated in radicalization pathways but are never the sole or most direct cause of radicalization. Furthermore, such factors are linked to many other life-course outcomes that do not involve ideological radicalization or joining extremist groups.[2]

2. Recruitment to radical groups deliberately leverages personal vulnerabilities, such as psychological distress and social marginalization.[3] Radical groups develop ways to bolster ideological commitment through restricting access to information or circumstances that challenge ideological constructs and through social and cognitive strategies for reinforcing in-group bias and hatred toward people outside the group.

3. Extremist groups nurture a self-reinforcing social milieu that includes shared purpose, camaraderie, friendship, and joint activities that involve both risk and emotional rewards.[4] Often, the thrill of violence and confrontation provides a ritual that bolsters group commitment.

4. Both the radicalization and the deradicalization process can be triggered by an individual's experience of a dramatic, challenging life event (e.g., death of a friend, life-threatening medical diagnosis, imprisonment) that causes them to

---

[1]   S. Rudenstine, A. Espinosa, A. B. McGee, and E. Routhier, "Adverse Childhood Events, Adult Distress, and the Role of Emotion Regulation," *Traumatology*, Vol. 25, No. 2, 2019.

[2]   Julia I. Herzog and Christian Schmahl, "Adverse Childhood Experiences and the Consequences on Neurobiological, Psychosocial, and Somatic Conditions Across the Lifespan," *Frontiers in Psychiatry*, Vol. 9, No. 420, September 2018. Also see Tiffany M. Jones, Paula Nurius, Chiho Song, and Christopher M. Fleming, "Modeling Life Course Pathways from Adverse Childhood Experiences to Adult Mental Health," *Child Abuse and Neglect*, Vol. 80, June 2018.

[3]   See Jensen, Seate, and James, 2020.

[4]   See Jensen, Seate, and James, 2020, p. 1070.

rethink their life circumstances and priorities.[5] Both radicalization and deradicalization often rely on other key individuals being in the right place at the right
time (and having the right relationship with the focal individual) to encourage
that individual to radicalize or deradicalize.

5. Radical ideology and involvement in extremist activities have addictive prop-
    erties for many,[6] whether such activities involve physical violence or trading
    insults online. These addictive properties appear linked to the experience of
    joint risk and struggle and likely involve core psychological rewards linked with
    thrill-seeking, righteous anger, and in-group belonging. As a result, support
    networks and "buddy systems" for deradicalizing and staying deradicalized
    appear to be crucial.

6. Attempts by formal institutions to deradicalize individuals sometimes work but
    often fail as well. In particular, heavy-handed attempts to derail radical activi-
    ties and groups by intelligence and law enforcement agencies—while under-
    standable to protect the public in many cases—can sometimes deepen ongoing
    radicalization processes and push potentially salvageable cases to more-extreme
    behaviors and involvement.[7]

7. Stigmatization of groups, whether Islamic, rural white, or otherwise, seems
    mostly to push individuals with risk for radicalization further down the extrem-
    ist path.[8] Punitive measures, banned speech, and indignant public discourse can
    backfire and increase the drive for radicalization.[9]

8. Media literacy and open access to diverse sources of information appear critical
    for deradicalization. In certain cases, structured interventions that involve expo-
    sure to people outside the group who exhibit kindness and generosity appear
    to have dramatic transformative effects. Such effects also occur, occasionally,
    through happenstance life events.

9. Although radical ideological movements rise and fall over time, split and join
    with each other, and reinvent themselves in new guises, their enduring appeal
    seems to lie in attending to fundamental human needs (for social bonds, love

---

[5] See Quintan Wiktorowicz, *Radical Islam Rising: Muslim Extremism in the West*, Lanham, Md.: Rowman &
Littlefield Publishers, 2005, p. 20.

[6] See Simi et al., 2017.

[7] See Lasse Lindekilde, "A Typology of Backfire Mechanisms," in Lorenzo Bosi, Chares Demetriou, and Stefan
Malthaner, eds., *Dynamics of Political Violence: A Process-Oriented Perspective on Radicalization and the Escalation
of Political Conflict*, London: Routledge, 2014.

[8] See Willem Koomen and Joop van der Pligt, *The Psychology of Radicalization and Terrorism*, New York: Routledge, 2015, pp. 12–23.

[9] See Lindekilde, 2014.

and acceptance,[10] meaning,[11] etc.) that sometimes go unmet. Meeting such needs through less destructive means is thus crucial.

Recommendations

On the basis of our literature review and interview analysis, we believe the following directions in research, policy, and practice are critical for research organizations, policymakers, and practitioners to pursue. We first present critical directions for future research, followed by changes to community policies and practices.

Research Directions

1. **Further develop and formally evaluate intervention approaches that former radicals themselves have created and that they currently employ informally.** Throughout our interviews, formers talked about extracting (or being extracted) from radical organizations by other formers who have developed their own homegrown approaches to helping others deradicalize. These should be scaled up and tested. Our interviews highlight five types of interventions that deserve further attention, including funding to expand, formalize, and evaluate impacts:

    a. *Addiction-based programs countering hate and radicalization, including buddy systems to deter radicalization relapse.* Such programs treat radical involvement as a lifelong struggle using a chronic disease model, which matches the subjective experiences of many of our participants.

    b. *Educational and outreach efforts to help recognize and address signs of radicalization.* Our research identified several early signs of radicalization that friends, family, and others are able to notice. Organizations made up of former radicals currently run helplines and other efforts to provide support to family members, friends, and others, as well as provide them with tools to recognize potential signs of radicalization and suggestions for when, where, and how to (and not to) intervene.

    c. *Social network approaches to deradicalization.* Formers described how they used their own social connections to find and approach individuals in radical organizations who might be ready to leave these organizations and deradicalize.

---

[10] For example, see Emma A. Renström, Hanna Bäck, and Holly M. Knapton, "Exploring a Pathway to Radicalization: The Effects of Social Exclusion and Rejection Sensitivity," *Group Processes and Intergroup Relations*, Vol. 23, No. 8, 2020.

[11] For example, see Koomen and van der Pligt, 2015.

     d. *Deliberate exposure to "optimal contact" with groups used as targets of hatred by radical groups.* Formers described strategic exposure to positive experiences with ethnic minorities or others whom radicals were taught to hate, creating sometimes transformative effects. Cross-group contact may, in fact, be an "essential" component of lasting change. However, there are conditions under which contact tends to lead to better outcomes and increasing recognition that cross-group friendship is especially important.[12]

     e. *Programs that create a safe, mentored space for individuals to freely express themselves and challenge each other's beliefs.* Former radicals described feeling marginalized and avoiding exposure to "mainstream" contexts after feeling stigmatized or targeted for their beliefs, leading to further radicalization in "niche" information environments. Ongoing work indicates that nonconfrontational challenges to incorrect beliefs are more productive than direct challenges or shaming.[13] To the extent that such spaces can be created and maintained online or in other contexts, they are likely to help disrupt radicalization.

2. **Use both data science and ethnographic research to understand current processes of online radicalization to extreme right- and left-wing groups.** Most of our respondents were exposed to extremist propaganda online, and the internet also helped facilitate identifying and joining formal extremist groups. Some existing research has used creative strategies to interview budding radical extremists and understand more about (or even challenge) their thought processes. Although much radical discourse can be found on existing social media and discussion forums, this content is often removed by platforms, such as Twitter, Facebook, and Reddit, and likely is only the surface layer of radicalization, with much of the ideological hardening and formal joining of organizations occurring in more-private conversations. Creative use of both online and offline interviewing and group observation will be needed to further understand these radicalization processes and how best to disrupt them.

3. **Conduct research on environmental (institutional and societal) influences of extremism.** Public health and demographic research is increasingly examining how institutional and societal factors, such as unemployment, segregation, and income inequality, are associated and might produce certain health outcomes, including obesity, drug misuse, and suicide. These forces were described either explicitly or implicitly in our case narratives and should similarly be explored as contributors to developing extremist ideologies, joining extremist groups, committing violence within these groups, or exiting these groups

---

[12] Pettigrew et al., 2011.

[13] See review of this research in Marcellino et al., forthcoming. For original sources, see, for example, Zollo et al., 2015. Also see Steffens et al., 2019.

successfully. Thus, policies not directly focused on preventing extremism but rather on creating adequate and equitable opportunities and social safety nets may be important for curbing extremism.

4. **Better identify geographic and demographic hot spots for radicalization to white supremacy and other radical ideologies.** Not all communities are equally at risk of violent extremism. Our interviews provided some hints as to possible dangerous environments for radicalization, including poor rural environments with recent demographic and economic change, prisons, and high-density urban environments. The population of the United States is too vast and the base rate of extremism too low to offer geographical conformity in detection and mitigation policies. It will hence be critical to more carefully identify community locales and demographic groups at risk of extremism and then ensure that those local governments and civil society organizations are properly oriented toward the risk and outfitted to properly address it.

Community Policies and Practices

1. **Consider carefully the trade-offs and the appropriate balance between punitive and "soft" law enforcement interventions.** Many of our respondents were critical of harsh legal interventions, which in some cases had the iatrogenic effect of solidifying or strengthening extremist views or networks. Although interdiction of ongoing violent plots is an obvious target for traditional law enforcement responses, notification regarding the ongoing radicalization of individuals may warrant a different response. Since the death of George Floyd and other such incidents, law enforcement in the United States is currently facing a reckoning of "hard" versus "soft" interdiction for criminal activity more broadly.[14] Such attention toward when, where, and how to intervene with individual cases and in communities could and should be focused on radicalization as well.

2. **Increase advertisements and public service announcements about existing resources for individuals who want to deradicalize,** including helplines,[15] support groups,[16] and related organizations.[17] We heard that for deradicalization to be effective, those willing to exit an extremist group must be approached by the right person with the right message at the right place and at the right time. Wide dissemination of information about organizations that can help these individuals and their families may help accelerate this process. These community-

---

[14] Jeffrey Hiday, Meagan Cahill, John S. Hollywood, Dulani Woods, and Bob Harrison, "Protests and Police Reform: Q&A with RAND Experts," *RAND Blog*, June 18, 2020.

[15] Parents for Peace, website, undated.

[16] Beyond Barriers, website, undated; Light upon Light, website, undated; Parallel Networks, website, undated.

[17] Museum of Tolerance, website, undated; Homeboy Industries, website, undated.

based organizations, most of which are founded by former radical extremists who have dedicated their lives to making positive change and deradicalizing others, also need financial support to sustain and expand their operations.

3. **Organize community-based educational opportunities**[18] **that cultivate media literacy**[19] **and responsible internet use.** The fragmented media landscape has presented some challenging issues for the participants, especially when it came to understanding fundamental differences in content quality and veracity. This made them more vulnerable to manipulation. Many former extremists told us directly that less sensationalistic media coverage and educational approaches that emphasized critical thinking could be helpful in preventing radicalization. Educational efforts may cover the role of rules, codes of ethics, and editorial processes in the media, as well as the value of research and fact-checking in assessing the reliability of media content. Guidelines on how to recognize propaganda, misinformation, and disinformation may also be helpful.

4. **Expand opportunities for mental health care.** More than half our sample evidenced a past mental health problem, which is significantly higher than the proportion found in the general population. Other studies have also hinted at a comorbidity issue. For example, Moonshot CVE, an organization dedicated to supporting internet-based CVE initiatives, has conducted online experiments suggesting that right-wing violent extremists and those seeking to enter such right-wing organizations are significantly more likely to click on mental health treatment advertisements.[20] Although it is not possible to establish the causal effect of mental illness on extremism, the plausibility may provide incentive to buttress mental health services in locales at high risk of extremist recruitment and activity. And targeting mental health care toward active extremist populations may provide an opportunity to directly support disengagement.

5. **Help at-risk parents and families recognize and react to signs of extremist radicalization and engagement.** A number of participants in this study highlighted examples of how their budding radicalization was signaled to family members, friends, and schools. Some signals, such as observing youth consuming extremist propaganda or wearing or showcasing extremist symbols and paraphernalia, serve as unambiguous signs of at least a dabbling interest in extremism. Others, including significant changes in behavior and social networks and engagement in other secretive activities, are more general and could indicate

---

[18] Gift of Our Wounds, "Serve 2 Unite: Now a Parents 4 Peace Initiative," webpage, undated.

[19] Alice Huguet, Jennifer Kavanagh, Garrett Baker, and Marjory S. Blumenthal, *Exploring Media Literacy Education as a Tool for Mitigating Truth Decay*, Santa Monica, Calif.: RAND Corporation, RR-3050-RC, 2019.

[20] In particular, Moonshot CVE experiments have shown that violent far-right audiences were 48 percent more likely to click on a mental health ad, while users who were looking to join or engage with violent far-right organizations were 115 percent more likely to click. See Moonshot CVE, "Mental Health and Violent Extremism," 2019.

the manifestation of various problems beyond radicalization, such as mental health problems. All these issues, however, require family and parental engagement. Efforts that can help at-risk families (or those families residing in locales at high risk of extremist recruitment and activity) identify and quickly respond to markers of extremism and other childhood behavioral problems may help reduce the risk of radicalization.

6. **Provide opportunities for expanding diversity exposure to those at risk of ideological radicalization.** Exposure to diverse populations played a critical role in helping deradicalize and reorient a number of formers in our study. This points to the proposition that such diversity-exposure efforts could be more systematically exploited to limit the risk of radicalization or possibly deradicalize already-extremist members. We note that diversity exposure has been a key component of community efforts to counter Islamic extremism. Several community and religious-based organizations have promoted interfaith engagement events that both served to undercut Islamophobic attitudes among non-Muslim participants and helped undercut the risk for extremism among the Muslim participants. Applying such an approach to countering white supremacy appears to have similar promising effects among formers in our sample.

Conclusion

Violent extremism is a growing, serious national security threat in the United States and elsewhere. Efforts ranging from federal policies to community activism will be needed to address this threat. These will include efforts to prevent individuals from developing radical beliefs and joining extremist groups, that identify and interrupt threats before they occur, that locate and hold accountable violent actors and motivators, and that help individuals seeking a way out of extremist groups to exit and deradicalize. Research is needed to inform the most-effective ways for achieving these goals. For this study, we spoke with individuals who had participated in such groups or had family members or friends participate. We gathered their narratives and analyzed the data systematically to identify themes and constructs that can inform effective policies and programs. We are pleased to see research on extremism growing to include more firsthand accounts and for this report to contribute to this expanding and critically important body of work.

Literature Review Methods and Scope

We began our literature review by conducting keyword searches on Google for "extremism," "radicalization," "deradicalization," "violent extremism," or "terrorism," plus "America" or "United States" and "interviews" or "data" or "analysis." We also searched for variations on these terms and ran a search for any studies focusing on "former" extremists, "white supremacists," or "Islamic extremists." We then searched more specifically for these terms in several databases of journals, including Taylor & Francis Online, JSTOR, and SAGE Journals.

Since this initial search yielded a very small pool of studies,[1] we expanded our search parameters slightly to include analyses of the information contained in the PIRUS database and studies based on this database. PIRUS, which is a database of "2,226 Islamist, far-left, far-right, and single-issue extremists who have radicalized to violent and non-violent extremism in the United States from 1948 through 2018,"[2] is arguably the most influential and comprehensive database on the topic of domestic radicalization. Although the database does not solely contain information from primary sources, it does include information from interviews with radicalized or formerly radicalized individuals and their family, friends, or associates.[3] Therefore, it serves as an important resource for our research.

---

[1] Without expanding the search criteria slightly to include the PIRUS database, there were only nine available studies that met the search criteria of (1) concerning U.S. citizens or those radicalized while residing in the United States and (2) including primary research. This number went down to seven studies when we excluded two studies that analyzed the same sample pools as other studies in our selected body of literature. Furthermore, within this set of nine studies, there was only one study that included interviews with members of the far left; all others concerned only white supremacists or other far-right groups. Moreover, none of the original nine studies included interviews or primary-source material on Islamic extremists. It was thus necessary to expand the search parameters to include a more representative body of literature.

[2] Michael Jensen, Patrick James, and Herbert Tinsley, "Profiles of Individual Radicalization in the United States: Preliminary Findings," College Park: National Consortium for the Study of Terrorism and Responses to Terrorism, University of Maryland, January 2015.

[3] According to the researchers who compiled PIRUS, "The PIRUS database includes 147 variable fields that contain detailed information on the individuals' criminal activities and/or violent plots, their relationships with extremist groups, their radicalization processes, their attachment to ideological milieus, and their demographic characteristics and personal histories. Sources referenced include newspaper articles, websites (e.g., government,

In scoping our literature review, we chose to exclude several types of sources. First, we elected to exclude studies that solely or primarily concern European citizens or citizens of other foreign countries beyond the United States, given our focus on domestic radicalization within the United States. We also excluded journalistic articles and interviews by media outlets. Although several news outlets have conducted interviews with defectors from ISIS and other terrorist organizations, we excluded these from our review because they typically do not have the same level of rigor and objectivity as the interviews and analysis conducted as part of academic studies. Finally, we excluded studies that drew only on secondary sources and did not include original research; as the bulk of our data for this study comes from interviews with formerly radicalized individuals, we deemed it most informative to review the findings of similar studies. The rationale for these search parameters was to review studies that were very similar in nature to our own, thus providing useful background and a frame of reference for this study. For this reason, we excluded studies that focused exclusively on non-U.S. populations; although we recognize that there is a rich body of literature on radicalization and deradicalization stemming from Europe, Canada, and myriad other countries,[4] our aim was to provide a summary of only the most directly relevant literature to provide readers with the necessary background but keep the focus on our original research efforts.

We encountered two key methodological challenges in conducting this literature review: The first concerns the limited number of studies of this nature, and the second concerns the reliability of the data provided in such studies (a challenge also noted by the authors of several of the studies). Through our literature search, we discovered that there are a limited number of studies that rely on original interviews with radicalized individuals or former extremists in the United States. The reason for the dearth of such studies seems to be linked to the second methodological issue; researchers have highlighted issues with both identifying and obtaining interviewees and the reliability of any such interviewees as sources.[5] Unsurprisingly, potential interviewees

---

terrorist group, watchdog groups, research institutes, personal information finder sites), secondary datasets, peer-reviewed academic articles, journalistic accounts including books and documentaries, court records, police reports, **witness transcribed interviews**, psychological evaluations/reports, and **information credited to the individual being researched (verified personal websites, autobiographies, social media accounts)**" (emphasis added). See Jensen et al., 2016, p. 8.

[4]   For some particularly useful accounts of domestic radicalization and deradicalization in Europe, see Dawson, 2017; Bakker, 2006. Several European studies provided analyses of radicalization mechanisms for foreign fighters, given the prevalence of this phenomenon in Europe (in terms of both outgoing and returning foreign fighters). Since this issue is not as pronounced in the United States, particularly for the white supremacist groups examined in this study, we have not conducted a rigorous review of this body of literature, although we acknowledge the importance of this trend in the context of international terrorism.

[5]   See, for instance, these reports that discuss the methodological issues with interviewing terrorists: John Horgan, "Interviewing the Terrorists: Reflections on Fieldwork and Implications for Psychological Research," *Behavioral Sciences of Terrorism and Political Aggression*, Vol. 4, No. 3, 2012; M. Nilsson, "Interviewing Jihadists:

are difficult to identify and locate, as well as to persuade to agree to participate in interviews, as these individuals often fear identification (by their former group and the general public), reprisal, stigmatization, and legal prosecution. Moreover, interviewees who are currently incarcerated, stuck in a foreign country seeking repatriation, or otherwise detained may be more readily identifiable or accessible but are likely not reliable sources (or are at least very biased and have incentive to lie). This issue with reliability of interviewees was a driving factor behind our decision to exclude media interviews. After applying all the above inclusion and exclusion criteria, we compiled and reviewed a body of 23 works of literature. Of the 23 examined works, 11 were studies based on original interviews with individuals radicalized in the United States, one was a report based on interviews with nonradicalized individuals from a community historically susceptible to high levels of radicalization (the Somali American community in Minneapolis–Saint Paul), and 11 were analyses of PIRUS data.

The authors of the studies in the first category collected data through detailed life-history interviews with former extremists. Although there were slight differences in methodology across the studies, researchers generally adopted a similar approach to interviews, employing a semistructured interview protocol designed to "elicit an in-depth life history to produce narratives that reflect the complexities and intersectionality of identity, ideology, and life experiences."[6] In one study, the authors describe the structure of the interviews they conducted with 89 former U.S. white supremacists in more detail, explaining:

> Subjects were asked to describe their childhood experiences as an initial starting point. The interviews included questions about broad phases of the subject's extremism, such as entry, involvement, and disengagement, with probes to encourage subjects to elaborate on aspects of their life histories. Subjects were periodically asked direct questions to focus on specific topic areas, but the interviews relied on an unstructured format intended to generate unsolicited data embedded in their personal narratives. Each interview concluded with more structured questions and scale items to collect comparable information across interviewees in terms of risk factors (e.g., history of child abuse, mental health problems), demographic information, and criminality.[7]

To recruit participants for interviews, most studies employed a snowball sampling technique, asking each individual interviewed for additional contact suggestions; this approach helped research teams access more individuals than they would otherwise

---

On the Importance of Drinking Tea and Other Methodological Considerations," *Studies in Conflict and Terrorism*, Vol. 41, No. 6, 2018.

[6] Simi et al., 2017.

[7] Simi et al., 2017.

have been able to, given the secretive and illicit nature of extremist circles.[8] Interviews generally lasted several hours and were recorded and transcribed in their entirety. Researchers independently analyzed the interviews by carefully reading the transcripts and identifying and coding themes and key takeaways (in accordance with a previously developed coding scheme). Researchers then discussed and cross-verified the coded results among the whole research team to compare findings, identify and resolve discrepancies, and bolster the reliability of the results.[9] Research teams behind several of the studies also "took a 10% random sample of cases and coded each case twice using separate individuals" and applied Krippendorff's alpha procedure to test the reliability of the coding results.[10] Other studies employed a grounded theory approach (or modified grounded theory approach) in which researchers "analyze qualitative data in order to develop theories 'grounded' within the data. . . . This technique involves the construction of themes and subthemes as the researcher reads each interview. Themes emerge from the interviews and the ongoing procedures, allowing the development and verification of central categories or 'codes.'"[11] Additionally, researchers in some studies complemented the interview data collection by collecting and coding relevant open-source data (e.g., news articles, legal documents, other data sets, other academic studies).[12]

The group of studies based on PIRUS data uses similar methodologies to analyze the data, with the clear difference that these studies did not collect original data and are analyzing information from a database rather than a set of interviews. The researchers who constructed the PIRUS database describe the data collection and coding process as follows:

> First, researchers used open-sources and extant START [Study of Terrorism and Responses to Terrorism] research products to collect a list of names and preliminary background information on approximately 4,000 individuals from various ideological milieus and time frames for possible inclusion in the dataset. Second, researchers coded each of these observations to determine whether the individuals should be included in the dataset using the inclusion criteria detailed below. Third, researchers coded the relevant background, contextual, and ideological information for a random sample of individuals who were selected for inclusion in the dataset. Random sampling techniques were used to maximize (although not guarantee) the representativeness of the dataset at all points in time that are covered by the project (see question below regarding the representativeness of the dataset).

---

[8] See, for example, Bubolz and Simi, 2015.

[9] See, for instance, Windisch, Ligon, and Simi, 2019; Gary LaFree, Bo Jiang, and Lauren C. Porter, "Prison and Violent Political Extremism in the United States," *Journal of Quantitative Criminology*, Vol. 36, 2020.

[10] Jasko, LaFree, and Kruglanski, 2017.

[11] Simi, Windisch, and Sporer, 2016.

[12] See, for example, Simi, Windisch, and Sporer, 2016.

The criteria coding and full coding stages occurred in multiple waves, thereby producing sub-sets of fully coded data that allowed for preliminary analysis in the initial phases of the project.[13]

To be included in the database, each of the profiled individuals had to have, in the judgment of the researchers, (1) radicalized in the United States, (2) have "espoused or currently espouse ideological motives," and (3) "show evidence that his or her behaviors are/were linked to the ideological motives he or she espoused/espouses."[14] Additionally, each individual had to meet at least one of the following criteria: (1) the individual was arrested or charged for committing an ideologically motivated crime, (2) the individual was indicted for an ideologically motivated crime, (3) the individual was killed in action while involved in extremist activity, (4) the individual was or is a member of a designated terrorist organization (per the U.S. Department of State's list), or (5) the individual is or was involved with an organization whose leaders have been indicted for an ideologically motivated crime.[15] The examined studies based on PIRUS data largely analyze specific samples or subsets of the PIRUS data to provide insights into a particular aspect of extremism. For instance, one study, "Contextualizing Disengagement: How Exit Barriers Shape the Pathways Out of Far-Right Extremism in the United States," extracted life-history information about 50 individuals in the PIRUS database who were identified as far-right extremists and employed "qualitative comparative analysis to show how push/pull factors combine to produce disengagement pathways within the context of barriers to exit."[16] Another study, "Cut from the Same Cloth? A Comparative Study of Domestic Extremists and Gang Members in the United States," developed a model that, drawing on PIRUS data and data from the National Longitudinal Survey of Youth 1997, "emphasizes explicit, spurious, and indirect linkages" between gang members and domestic extremists.[17] In another study, "Prison and Violent Political Extremism in the United States," researchers explained: "[We] perform a two-stage analysis where we first preprocess the data using a matching technique to approximate a fully blocked experimental design. Using the matched data, we then calculate the conditional odds ratio for engaging in violent extremism and estimate

---

[13] Jensen et al., 2016.

[14] National Consortium for the Study of Terrorism and Responses to Terrorism, University of Maryland, "PIRUS—Frequently Asked Questions," webpage, undated-b.

[15] National Consortium for the Study of Terrorism and Responses to Terrorism, University of Maryland, undated-b.

[16] Jensen, James, and Yates, 2020.

[17] David C. Pyrooz, Gary LaFree, Scott H. Decker, and Patrick A. James, "Cut from the Same Cloth? A Comparative Study of Domestic Extremists and Gang Members in the United States," *Justice Quarterly*, Vol. 35, No. 1, 2018.

average treatment effects (ATE) of our outcomes of interest."[18] The rest of the studies in this category relied on a variety of other similar qualitative methods.

The study that examined factors contributing to potential vulnerability to radicalization in the Somali American community in Minneapolis–Saint Paul relied on interviews with 57 individuals "who were either: 1) Somali-American young adult males (ages 16 to 30) (n=18); 2) Somali-American parents or adult family members (n=19); or 3) service providers who work with the Somali community (n=20)."[19] Researchers recruited the interviewees through personal connections in the community of interest. The interviews were conducted by a team consisting of two American psychiatrists and three Somali Americans from the Minneapolis–Saint Paul community and in a similar manner to the other interview-based studies. Rather than life-history interviews, though, these interviews focused on the topics of "1) family and community protective processes with respect to violent extremism; 2) community knowledge and attitudes towards violent extremism; 3) the individual, family, and community processes underlying risks of violent extremism; 4) the potential role of lack of social integration in violent extremism; and 5) community knowledge, attitudes, and behaviors towards law enforcement."[20] The study used a grounded-theory approach to analyze the interview data.

---

[18] LaFree, Jiang, and Porter, 2020.

[19] Weine and Ahmed, 2012.

[20] Weine and Ahmed, 2012.

Interview Protocols

Focal Individual Protocol

This is a study funded by the National Institute of Justice to explore the reasons why people are recruited into organizations that are involved in violent activities against other groups or individuals.

As part of this study, we are interviewing friends and loved ones to better understand how they have experienced their loved one's changes—as well as individuals who have been involved in these organizations and are not involved any longer. The goal of this work is to develop a toolkit that can be used to help families and communities identify and redirect individuals who might be experiencing similar changes or challenges in their lives.

I would like to stress that your participation in this discussion is completely voluntary. We can stop at any point or skip any question. There are no consequences if you decline to participate or decline to answer any question during our conversation.

The interview will take approximately 60 minutes. I'll be taking notes on the call, though we usually record these conversations to help supplement our notes and make sure that we don't miss or misinterpret anything you say.

Risks of participation include the possibility for experiencing psychological distress while talking about your or your loved one's involvement with extremist groups. All private, identifiable information will be kept confidential and will only be used for research and statistical purposes. Deidentified data (isolated text records of some quotations from the interview with all names, place names, and other details that could be used to identify you removed) will be archived with National Archive of Criminal Justice Data or NIJ's designated repository.

While there are no direct benefits of participation, by helping us with this study, you will contribute to the development of a toolkit to help families and communities identify and redirect individuals who might be experiencing changes or challenges similar to those of you or your loved one. RAND will use the information you provide for research purposes only and your responses will be kept confidential and secure. Your name won't be linked or attributed to any of the information you provide us today. All of this information is kept securely at RAND. No one outside of the RAND research team will have access to the notes, recordings, or any other information we collect today, and all those materials will be destroyed at the end of the study.

I have just a little bit of background on your story from what is publicly available. Please tell me your story in your own words, and from your own perspective. I'd like to know what you remember about your early life, and then the events that led you to being part of this study. Please highlight major turning points or changes along the way. *[Interviewer: Make sure to cover the following areas: early life → radicalization process → focal event → deradicalization (if applicable).]*

- *Early life and characteristics*
  - What was your life like as a child?
  - How would you describe your personality? Your interests?
  - What about your family relationships and friendships?
  - What about your relationship to school, church/mosque, or any other institutions you were involved in?
- *Major warning signals and turning points*
  - When did you experience a change in your own perspective?
  - What stands out to you as a sign that others might see changed about you during this time?
- *Attempts to intervene*
  - Did any friends, family members, or others say notice these and say anything to you about them? If so, how did you respond to them?
  - What sort of help or advice do you wish you had, in retrospect?
- *Focal event*
  - Please tell me what happened next. *[Interviewer: If necessary, prompt with additional details, such as, "Can you please tell me about becoming associated with (GROUP NAME)?"]*
- *Current status*
  - How are you doing today? What are you looking forward to in your future?
- *Deradicalization (if applicable):*
  - How did you leave [GROUP NAME] or change their perspective?
  - What do you think helped you make these changes?

Thank you. Now, I'd like to ask for you to tell me about the things that you think helped lead to these events. You can talk about anything that comes to mind; these can be people, institutions, experiences, aspects of your personality . . . anything that you think is important! We may have covered some of these already, but that's OK. *[Interviewer: Probe for the following areas unless they come up naturally. Also, after each item the respondent lists, ask them to explain a bit about how they think this was causally related.]*

- *Personal characteristics: personality, early experiences, mental or physical health*
- *Core radical organization and recruiters/foot soldiers*
- *Community context*
- *Traumatic or stressful life event(s)*
- *Struggle with identity*
- *Law enforcement/criminal justice system*
- *Religious institutions*
- *School/university*
- *Job/employment*
- *Friends*
- *Family*
- *Online*

Thank you for that. [IF APPLICABLE:] So, on the opposite side of things, can you please tell me about all the things that you think helped you leave [GROUP NAME]? As with the previous question, you can talk about anything that comes to mind. *[Interviewer: Probe as needed using bulleted list above. As before, ask the respondent to provide a short causal narrative for each item listed.]*

Thank you for going into so much detail. I have another question for you. What can you think of that might have helped prevent this? Again, anything goes here. We want your ideas, even if they would be difficult to implement.

Finally, what else do you think is important for me to know or that we didn't have a chance to discuss today?

Family Member or Friend Protocol

This is a study funded by the National Institute of Justice to explore the reasons why people are recruited into organizations that are involved in violent activities against other groups or individuals.

As part of this study, we are interviewing friends and loved ones to better understand how they have experienced their loved one's changes—as well as individuals who have been involved in these organizations and are not involved any longer. The goal of this work is to develop a toolkit that can be used to help families and communities identify and redirect individuals who might be experiencing similar changes or challenges in their lives.

I would like to stress that your participation in this discussion is completely voluntary. We can stop at any point or skip any question. There are no consequences if you decline to participate or decline to answer any question during our conversation.

The interview will take approximately 60 minutes. I'll be taking notes on the call, though we usually record these conversations to help supplement our notes and make sure that we don't miss or misinterpret anything you say.

Risks of participation include the possibility for experiencing psychological distress while talking about your or your loved one's involvement with extremist groups. All private, identifiable information will be kept confidential and will only be used for research and statistical purposes. Deidentified data (isolated text records of some quotations from the interview with all names, place names, and other details that could be used to identify you removed) will be archived with National Archive of Criminal Justice Data or NIJ's designated repository.

While there are no direct benefits of participation, by helping us with this study, you will contribute to the development of a toolkit to help families and communities identify and redirect individuals who might be experiencing changes or challenges similar to those of you or your loved one. RAND will use the information you provide for research purposes only and your responses will be kept confidential and secure. Your name won't be linked or attributed to any of the information you provide us today. All of this information is kept securely at RAND. No one outside of the RAND research team will have access to the notes, recordings, or any other information we collect today, and all those materials will be destroyed at the end of the study.

I have just a little bit of background on the story of [NAME] from what is publicly available. Please tell me the story of [NAME]. I want to hear this in your own words, and from your own perspective. I'd like to know what you remember about [NAME'S] early life, and then the events involving [him/her] that led you to being part of this study. Please highlight major turning points, changes, or warning signals you observed along the way. Please also describe any efforts you and others made to help [NAME] along the way. *[Interviewer: Make sure to cover the following areas: Early life → radicalization process → focal event → deradicalization (if applicable).]*

- *Early life and characteristics*
  - What was [NAME] like as a child?
  - How would you describe their personality? How would you describe their interests?
  - What about their family relationships and friendships?
  - What about their relationship to school, church/mosque, or any other institutions they were involved in?
- *Major warning signals and turning points*
  - When did you first notice that something had changed in their personality or behaviors? What did you notice? How did you notice this?
  - What stands out to you as a sign that something was different about [NAME] during this time?

- *Attempts to intervene*
  - Did you say anything to [NAME] when you noticed these changes? Do you know if anyone else said anything to [NAME]? What did they do?
  - How did [NAME] respond to you/them?
  - Is there anything you think that you would have done differently? What is it? Why do you think that?
  - What sort of help or advice do you wish you had, in retrospect?
- *Focal event*
  - Please tell me what happened next. *[Interviewer: If necessary, prompt with additional details, such as, "Can you please tell me about (NAME) becoming associated with (GROUP NAME)?"]*
  - How did you know that your loved one was in trouble?
- *Current status*
  - How is [NAME] doing today? What are the prospects for their future?
- *Deradicalization (if applicable)*
  - How did [NAME] leave [GROUP NAME], or change their perspective?
  - What do you think helped [NAME] make these changes?

Thank you. Now, I'd like to ask for you to tell me about the things that you think helped lead to the events involving your loved one. You can talk about anything that comes to mind; these can be people, institutions, experiences, aspects of [NAME]'s personality . . . anything that you think is important! We may have covered some of these already, but that's OK. *[Interviewer: Probe for the following areas unless they come up naturally. Also, after each item the respondent lists, ask them to explain a bit about how they think this was causally related.]*

- *Personal characteristics: personality, early experiences, mental or physical health*
- *Core radical organization and recruiters/foot soldiers*
- *Community context*
- *Traumatic or stressful life event(s)*
- *Struggle with identity*
- *Law enforcement/criminal justice system*
- *Religious institutions*
- *School/university*
- *Job/employment*
- *Friends*
- *Family*
- *Online*

Thank you for that. [IF APPLICABLE:] So, on the opposite side of things, can you please tell me about all the things that you think helped [NAME] leave [GROUP

NAME]? As with the previous question, you can talk about anything that comes to mind. *[Interviewer, probe as needed using the bulleted list above. As before, ask the respondent to provide a short causal narrative for each item listed.]*

Thank you for going into so much detail. I have another question for you. What can you think of that might have helped prevent this? Again, anything goes here. We want your ideas, even if they would be difficult to implement.

Finally, what else do you think is important for me to know or that we didn't have a chance to discuss today?

References

Ahmed, Kawser, "Radicalism Leading to Violent Extremism in Canada: A Multi-Level Analysis of Muslim Community and University Based Student Leaders' Perceptions and Experiences," *Journal for Deradicalization*, No. 6, Spring 2016, pp. 231–271.

Aldrich, D. P., "First Steps Towards Hearts and Minds? USAID's Countering Violent Extremism Policies in Africa," *Terrorism and Political Violence*, Vol. 26, No. 3, 2014, pp. 523–546.

Allport, Gordon W., *The Nature of Prejudice*, Reading, Mass.: Addison-Wesley, 1979.

Anti-Defamation League, "White Aryan Resistance," webpage, undated. As of March 7, 2021:
https://www.adl.org/education/references/hate-symbols/white-aryan-resistance

———, *The Sounds of Hate: The White Power Music Scene in the United States in 2012*, New York, 2012. As of February 10, 2021:
https://www.adl.org/sites/default/files/documents/assets/pdf/combating-hate/
Sounds-of-Hate-White-Power-Music-Scene-2012.pdf

Arnstein, S. R., "A Ladder of Citizen Participation," *Journal of the American Institute of Planners*, Vol. 35, No. 4, 1969, pp. 216–224.

Azrael, Deborah, and Matthew J. Miller, "Reducing Suicide Without Affecting Underlying Mental Health," in Rory C. O'Connor and Jane Pirkis, eds., *The International Handbook of Suicide Prevention*, 2nd ed., Hoboken, N.J.: Wiley Blackwell, 2016, pp. 637–662.

Bakker, Edwin, *Jihadi Terrorists in Europe: Their Characteristics and the Circumstances in Which They Joined the Jihad; An Exploratory Study*, Clingendael: Netherlands Institute of International Relations, December 2006.

Balch, R. W., "When the Light Goes Out, Darkness Comes: A Study of Defection from a Totalistic Cult," in R. Stark, ed., *Religious Movements: Genesis, Exodus, and Numbers*, New York: Paragon House, 1986, pp. 11–63.

Beaghley, Sina, Todd C. Helmus, Miriam Matthews, Rajeev Ramchand, David Stebbins, Amanda Kadlec, and Michael A. Brown, *Development and Pilot Test of the RAND Program Evaluation Toolkit for Countering Violent Extremism*, Santa Monica, Calif.: RAND Corporation, RR-1799-DHS, 2017. As of February 23, 2021:
https://www.rand.org/pubs/research_reports/RR1799.html

Bernard, H. Russell, and Gery W. Ryan, "Text Analysis Qualitative and Quantitative Methods," in H. Russell Bernard, ed., *Handbook of Methods in Cultural Anthropology*, Walnut Creek, Calif.: AltaMira Press, 1998, pp. 595–646.

Beyond Barriers, website, undated. As of January 20, 2021:
https://beyondbarriersusa.org/

Bharath, Deepa, "Organization of Former Extremists Gets $750,000 from DHS to Counter Threats from the Far Right," *Orange County Register*, October 4, 2020. As of February 10, 2021:
https://www.ocregister.com/2020/10/03/
organization-of-former-extremists-gets-750000-from-dhs-to-counter-threats-from-the-far-right/

Bhui, Kamaldeep S., Madelyn H. Hicks, Myrna Lashley, and Edgar Jones, "A Public Health Approach to Understanding and Preventing Violent Radicalization," *BMC Medicine*, Vol. 10, No. 1, 2012.

Bubolz, Bryan F., and Pete Simi, "Leaving the World of Hate: Life-Course Transitions and Self-Change," *American Behavioral Scientist*, Vol. 59, No. 2, 2015, pp. 1588–1608.

Cavanagh, J. T. O., A. J. Carson, M. Sharpe, and S. M. Lawrie, "Psychological Autopsy Studies of Suicide: A Systematic Review," *Psychological Medicine*, Vol. 33, No. 3, 2003, pp. 395–405.

CDC—*See* Centers for Disease Control and Prevention.

Centers for Disease Control and Prevention, "The Social-Ecological Model: A Framework for Prevention," webpage, last reviewed January 28, 2021. As of February 23, 2021:
https://www.cdc.gov/violenceprevention/about/social-ecologicalmodel.html

Centre for Justice Reconciliation, "Lesson 1: What Is Restorative Justice?" webpage, undated. As of January 21, 2021:
http://restorativejustice.org/restorative-justice/about-restorative-justice/
tutorial-intro-to-restorative-justice/lesson-1-what-is-restorative-justice

Conner, Kenneth R., Annette L. Beautrais, David A. Brent, Yeates Conwell, Michael R. Phillips, and Barbara Schneider, "The Next Generation of Psychological Autopsy Studies: Part I. Interview Content," *Suicide and Life-Threatening Behavior*, Vol. 41, No. 6, 2011, pp. 594–613.

Corner, Emily, and Paul Gill, "Is There a Nexus Between Terrorist Involvement and Mental Health in the Age of the Islamic State?" *CTC Sentinel*, Vol. 10, No. 1, 2017, pp. 1–10.

Cotter, John M., "Sounds of Hate: White Power Rock and Roll and the Neo-Nazi Skinhead Subculture," *Terrorism and Political Violence*, Vol. 11, No. 2, 1999, pp. 111–140.

Dahlberg, Linda L., and Etienne G. Krug, "Violence: A Global Public Health Problem," in Etienne G. Krug, Linda L. Dahlberg, James A. Mercy, Anthony B. Zwi, and Rafael Lozano, eds., *World Report on Violence and Health*, Geneva: World Health Organization, 2002, pp. 1–21.

Davis, Paul K., and Kim Cragin, eds., *Social Science for Counterterrorism: Putting the Pieces Together*, Santa Monica, Calif.: RAND Corporation, MG-849-OSD, 2009. As of February 16, 2021:
https://www.rand.org/pubs/monographs/MG849.html

Dawson, Lorne L., *Sketch of a Social Ecology Model for Explaining Homegrown Terrorist Radicalisation*, The Hague, Netherlands: International Centre for Counter-Terrorism—The Hague, 2017.

Dawson, Lorne L., and Amarnath Amarasingam, "Talking to Foreign Fighters: Insights into the Motivations for Hijrah to Syria and Iraq," *Studies in Conflict and Terrorism*, Vol. 40, No. 3, 2017, pp. 191–210.

Falk, Armin, Andreas Kuhn, and Josef Zweimüller, "Unemployment and Right-Wing Extremist Crime," *Scandinavian Journal of Economics*, Vol. 113, No. 2, 2011, pp. 260–285.

Feddes, Allard Rienk, Liesbeth Mann, Bertjan Doosje, "Increasing Self-Esteem and Empathy to Prevent Violent Radicalization: A Longitudinal Quantitative Evaluation of a Resilience Training Focused on Adolescents with a Dual Identity," *Journal of Applied Social Psychology*, Vol. 45, No. 7, 2015, pp. 400–411.

Federal Bureau of Investigation, "What Is Violent Extremism?" "Don't Be a Puppet" website, undated. As of January 17, 2021:
https://www.fbi.gov/cve508/teen-website/what-is-violent-extremism

Frenett, Ross, and Moli Dow, *One to One Online Interventions: A Pilot CVE Methodology*, London: Institute for Strategic Dialogue and Curtain University, 2014. As of February 10, 2021:
https://www.isdglobal.org/isd-publications/one-to-one-online-interventions-a-pilot-cve-methodology/

Futrell, Robert, Pete Simi, and Simon Gottschalk, "Understanding Music in Movements: The White Power Music Scene," *Sociological Quarterly*, Vol. 47, No. 2, 2006, pp. 275–304.

Gift of Our Wounds, "Serve 2 Unite: Now a Parents 4 Peace Initiative," webpage, undated. As of January 20, 2021:
https://www.giftofourwounds.com/serve2unite

Gill, Paul, Caitlin Clemmow, Florian Hetzel, Bettina Rottweiler, Nadine Salman, Isabelle van der Vegt, Zoe Marchment, Sandy Schumann, Sanaz Zolghadriha, Norah Schulten, Helen Taylor, and Emily Corner, "Systematic Review of Mental Health Problems and Violent Extremism," *Journal of Forensic Psychiatry and Psychology*, Vol. 32, No. 1, 2021, pp. 51–78.

Hamm, Mark, and Ramon Spaaij, "Lone Wolf Terrorism in America: Using Knowledge of Radicalization Pathways to Forge Prevention Strategies," Indiana State University, 2015.

Hegghammer, Thomas, "Terrorist Recruitment and Radicalization in Saudi Arabia," *Middle East Policy*, Vol. 13, No. 4, 2006, pp. 39–60.

Helmus, Todd C., "Why and How Some People Become Terrorists," in Paul K. Davis and Kim Cragin, eds., *Social Science for Counterterrorism: Putting the Pieces Together*, Santa Monica, Calif.: RAND Corporation, MG-849-OSD, 2008, pp. 71–112. As of February 10, 2021:
http://www.rand.org/pubs/monographs/MG849.html

Helmus, Todd C., Erin York, and Peter Chalk, *Promoting Online Voices for Countering Violent Extremism*, Santa Monica, Calif.: RAND Corporation, RR-130-OSD, 2013. As of February 19, 2021:
https://www.rand.org/pubs/research_reports/RR130.html

Henderson-King, Donna, Eaaron Henderson-King, Bryan Bolea, Kurt Koches, and Amy Kauffman, "Seeking Understanding or Sending Bombs: Beliefs as Predictors of Responses to Terrorism," *Peace and Conflict*, Vol. 10, No. 1, 2004, pp. 67–84.

Herzog, Julia I., and Christian Schmahl, "Adverse Childhood Experiences and the Consequences on Neurobiological, Psychosocial, and Somatic Conditions Across the Lifespan," *Frontiers in Psychiatry*, Vol. 9, No. 420, September 2018.

Hiday, Jeffrey, Meagan Cahill, John S. Hollywood, Dulani Woods, and Bob Harrison, "Protests and Police Reform: Q&A with RAND Experts," *RAND Blog*, June 18, 2020. As of January 20, 2021:
https://www.rand.org/blog/2020/06/protests-and-police-reform-qampa-with-rand-experts.html

Homeboy Industries, website, undated. As of January 20, 2021:
https://homeboyindustries.org/

Horgan, John, "Interviewing the Terrorists: Reflections on Fieldwork and Implications for Psychological Research," *Behavioral Sciences of Terrorism and Political Aggression*, Vol. 4, No. 3, 2012, pp. 195–211.

Horgan, John, Mary Beth Altier, Neil Shortland, and Max Taylor, "Walking Away: The Disengagement and De-Radicalization of a Violent Right-Wing Extremist," *Behavioral Sciences of Terrorism and Political Aggression*, Vol. 9, No. 2, May 2017, pp. 63–77.

Huguet, Alice, Jennifer Kavanagh, Garrett Baker, and Marjory S. Blumenthal, *Exploring Media Literacy Education as a Tool for Mitigating Truth Decay*, Santa Monica, Calif.: RAND Corporation, RR-3050-RC, 2019. As of February 23, 2021:
https://www.rand.org/pubs/research_reports/RR3050.html

Jackson, Brian A., Ashley L. Rhoades, Jordan R. Reimer, Natasha Lander, Katherine Costello, and Sina Beaghley, "Building an Effective and Practical National Approach to Terrorism Prevention," Homeland Security Operational Analysis Center operated by the RAND Corporation, RB-10030-DHS, 2019a. As of February 23, 2021:
https://www.rand.org/pubs/research_briefs/RB10030.html

———, *Practical Terrorism Prevention: Reexamining U.S. National Approaches to Addressing the Threat of Ideologically Motivated Violence*, Homeland Security Operational Analysis Center operated by the RAND Corporation, RR-2647-DHS, 2019b. As of February 23, 2021:
https://www.rand.org/pubs/research_reports/RR2647.html

Jasko, Katarzyna, Gary LaFree, and Arie Kruglanski, "Quest for Significance and Violent Extremism: The Case of Domestic Radicalization," *Political Psychology*, Vol. 38, No. 5, 2017, pp. 815–831.

Jenkins, Brian Michael, "The Battle of Capitol Hill," *RAND Blog*, January 11, 2021. As of January 19, 2021:
https://www.rand.org/blog/2021/01/the-battle-of-capitol-hill.html

Jensen, Michael, Patrick James, Gary LaFree, and Aaron Safer-Lichtenstein, "Pre-Radicalization Criminal Activity of United States Extremists," College Park: National Consortium for the Study of Terrorism and Responses to Terrorism, University of Maryland, January 2018.

Jensen, Michael, Patrick James, Gary LaFree, Aaron Safer-Lichtenstein, and Elizabeth Yates, *The Use of Social Media by United States Extremists*, College Park: National Consortium for the Study of Terrorism and Responses to Terrorism, University of Maryland, 2018.

Jensen, Michael, Patrick James, and Herbert Tinsley, "Profiles of Individual Radicalization in the United States: Preliminary Findings," College Park: National Consortium for the Study of Terrorism and Responses to Terrorism, University of Maryland, January 2015.

Jensen, Michael, Patrick James, and Elizabeth Yates, "Contextualizing Disengagement: How Exit Barriers Shape the Pathways Out of Far-Right Extremism in the United States," *Studies in Conflict and Terrorism*, May 4, 2020.

Jensen, Michael, Gary LaFree, Patrick A. James, Anita Atwell-Seate, Daniela Pisoiu, John Stevenson, and Herbert Tinsley, *Empirical Assessment of Domestic Radicalization (EADR)*, College Park: National Consortium for the Study of Terrorism and Responses to Terrorism, University of Maryland, 2016.

Jensen, Michael A., Anita Atwell Seate, and Patrick A. James, "Radicalization to Violence: A Pathway Approach to Studying Extremism," *Terrorism and Political Violence*, Vol. 32, No. 5, July 2020, pp. 1067–1090.

Johns, Amelia, Michele Grossman, and Kevin McDonald, "'More Than a Game': The Impact of Sport-Based Youth Mentoring Schemes on Developing Resilience Toward Violent Extremism," *Social Inclusion*, Vol. 2, No. 2, 2014, pp. 57–70.

Jones, Seth G., Catrina Doxsee, and Nicholas Harring, "The Escalating Terrorism Problem in the United States," Center for Strategic and International Studies, June 17, 2020.

Jones, Tiffany M., Paula Nurius, Chiho Song, and Christopher M. Fleming, "Modeling Life Course Pathways from Adverse Childhood Experiences to Adult Mental Health," *Child Abuse and Neglect*, Vol. 80, June 2018, pp. 32–40.

Koomen, Willem, and Joop van der Pligt, *The Psychology of Radicalization and Terrorism*, New York: Routledge, 2015.

Krueger, Alan B., and Jitka Malečková, "Education, Poverty and Terrorism: Is There a Causal Connection?" *Journal of Economic Perspectives*, Vol. 17, No. 4, 2003, pp. 119–144.

LaFree, Gary, Michael A. Jensen, Patrick A. James, and Aaron Safer-Lichtenstein, "Correlates of Violent Political Extremism in the United States," *Criminology*, Vol. 56, No. 2, 2018, pp. 233–268.

LaFree, Gary, Bo Jiang, and Lauren C. Porter, "Prison and Violent Political Extremism in the United States," *Journal of Quantitative Criminology*, Vol. 36, 2020, pp. 473–498.

Light Upon Light, website, undated. As of January 20, 2021:
https://www.lightuponlight.online/

Lindekilde, Lasse, "A Typology of Backfire Mechanisms," in Lorenzo Bosi, Chares Demetriou, and Stefan Malthaner, eds., *Dynamics of Political Violence: A Process-Oriented Perspective on Radicalization and the Escalation of Political Conflict*, London: Routledge, 2014, pp. 51–69.

MacQueen, Kathleen M., Eleanor McLellan, Kelly Kay, and Bobby Milstein, "Codebook Development for Team-Based Qualitative Analysis," *Cultural Anthropology Methods*, Vol. 10, No. 2, 1998, pp. 31–36.

Marcellino, William, Todd C. Helmus, Joshua Kerrigan, Hilary Reininger, Rouslan I. Karimov, and Rebecca Ann Lawrence, *Detecting Conspiracy Theories on Social Media: Improving Machine Learning to Detect and Understand Conspiracy Theories*, Santa Monica, Calif.: RAND Corporation, RR-A676-1, forthcoming.

McGilloway, A., P. Ghosh, and K. Bhui, "A Systematic Review of Pathways to and Processes Associated with Radicalization and Extremism Amongst Muslims in Western Societies," *International Review of Psychiatry*, Vol. 27, No. 1, 2015, pp. 39–50.

Merriam-Webster, "White Supremacist," undated. As of February 7, 2021:
https://www.merriam-webster.com/dictionary/white%20supremacist

Moonshot CVE, "Mental Health and Violent Extremism," 2019. As of January 20, 2021:
https://moonshotcve.com/wp-content/uploads/2019/07/
Moonshot-CVE-Mental-Health-and-Violent-Extremism.pdf

Museum of Tolerance, website, undated. As of January 20, 2021:
https://www.museumoftolerance.com/

National Academies of Sciences, Engineering, and Medicine, *Countering Violent Extremism Through Public Health Practice: Proceedings of a Workshop*, Washington, D.C.: National Academies Press, 2017.

National Consortium for the Study of Terrorism and Responses to Terrorism, University of Maryland, Profiles of Individual Radicalization in the United States, database, undated-a. As of March 1, 2021:
https://start.umd.edu/data-tools/profiles-individual-radicalization-united-states-pirus

———, "PIRUS—Frequently Asked Questions," webpage, undated-b. As of January 24, 2021:
https://www.start.umd.edu/pirus-frequently-asked-questions

———, "Profiles of Individual Radicalization in the United States (PIRUS)," College Park, May 2020.

National Institute of Mental Health, "Mental Illness," webpage, last updated January 2021. As of March 1, 2021:
https://www.nimh.nih.gov/health/statistics/mental-illness.shtml

National Institute of Justice, "Research Provides Guidance on Building Effective Counterterrorism Programs," July 8, 2018. As of November 14, 2020:
https://nij.ojp.gov/topics/articles/research-provides-guidance-building-effective-counterterrorism-programs

Neumann, P., and S. Kleinmann, "How Rigorous Is Radicalization Research?" *Democracy and Security*, Vol. 9, No. 4, 2013, pp. 360–382.

Nilsson, M., "Interviewing Jihadists: On the Importance of Drinking Tea and Other Methodological Considerations," *Studies in Conflict and Terrorism*, Vol. 41, No. 6, 2018, pp. 419–432.

Oxford University Press, "Definition of Extremism in English," Lexico.com, 2020a. As of January 17, 2021:
https://www.lexico.com/en/definition/extremism

———, "Definition of Radicalization in English," Lexico.com, 2020b. As of January 17, 2021:
https://www.lexico.com/en/definition/radicalization

———, "Definition of Terrorism in English," Lexico.com, 2020c. As of January 17, 2021:
https://www.lexico.com/en/definition/terrorism

Parallel Networks, website, undated. As of January 20, 2021:
http://pnetworks.org/

Parents for Peace, website, undated. As of January 20, 2021:
https://www.parents4peace.org

Pettigrew, Thomas F., Linda R. Tropp, Ulrich Wagner, and Oliver Christ, "Recent Advances in Intergroup Contact Theory," *International Journal of Intercultural Relations*, Vol. 35, 2011, pp. 271–280.

Pyrooz, David C., Gary LaFree, Scott H. Decker, and Patrick A. James, "Cut from the Same Cloth? A Comparative Study of Domestic Extremists and Gang Members in the United States," *Justice Quarterly*, Vol. 35, No. 1, 2018, pp. 1–32.

Ramchand, Rajeev, Enchanté Franklin, Elizabeth Thornton, Sarah Deland, and Jeffrey Rouse, "Opportunities to Intervene? 'Warning Signs' for Suicide in the Days Before Dying," *Death Studies*, Vol. 41, No. 6, 2017, pp. 368–375.

Renström, Emma A., Hanna Bäck, and Holly M. Knapton, "Exploring a Pathway to Radicalization: The Effects of Social Exclusion and Rejection Sensitivity," *Group Processes and Intergroup Relations*, Vol. 23, No. 8, 2020, pp. 1204–1229.

Rhoades, Ashley L., and Todd C. Helmus, *Countering Violent Extremism in the Philippines: A Snapshot of Current Challenges and Responses*, Santa Monica, Calif.: RAND Corporation, RR-A233-2, 2020. As of January 21, 2021:
https://www.rand.org/pubs/research_reports/RRA233-2.html

Rhoades, Ashley L., Todd C. Helmus, James V. Marrone, Victoria M. Smith, and Elizabeth Bodine-Baron, *Promoting Peace as the Antidote to Violent Extremism: Evaluation of a Philippines-Based Tech Camp and Peace Promotion Fellowship*, Santa Monica, Calif.: RAND Corporation, RR-A233-3, 2020. As of January 21, 2021:
https://www.rand.org/pubs/research_reports/RRA233-3.html

Robertson, Campbell, Christopher Mele, and Sabrina Tavernise, "11 Killed in Synagogue Massacre; Suspect Charged with 29 Counts," *New York Times*, October 27, 2018.

Rudenstine, S., A. Espinosa, A. B. McGee, and E. Routhier, "Adverse Childhood Events, Adult Distress, and the Role of Emotion Regulation," *Traumatology*, Vol. 25, No. 2, 2019, pp. 124–132.

Ryan, Gery W., and H. Russell Bernard, "Techniques to Identify Themes," *Field Methods*, Vol. 15, No. 1, 2003, pp. 85–109.

Sageman, Marc, *Leaderless Jihad: Terror Networks in the Twenty-First Century*, Philadelphia: University of Pennsylvania Press, 2008.

———, "The Stagnation in Terrorism Research," *Terrorism and Political Violence*, Vol. 26, No. 4, 2014, pp. 565–580.

Schuurman, Bart, "Research on Terrorism, 2007–2016: A Review of Data, Methods, and Authorship," *Terrorism and Political Violence*, Vol. 32, No. 5, 2018, pp. 1011–1026.

Schuurman, Bart, and Quirine Eijkman, *Moving Terrorism Research Forward: The Crucial Role of Primary Sources*, The Hague, Netherlands: International Centre for Counter-Terrorism—The Hague, 2013.

Sciolino, Elaine, and Eric Schmitt, "A Not Very Private Feud over Terrorism," *New York Times*, June 8, 2008.

Scrivens, Ryan, Vivek Venkatesh, Maxime Bérubé, and Tiana Gaudette, "Combating Violent Extremism: Voices of Former Right-Wing Extremists," *Studies in Conflict and Terrorism*, November 11, 2019.

Simi, Pete, Kathleen Blee, Matthew DeMichele, and Steven Windisch, "Addicted to Hate: Identity Residual Among Former White Supremacists," *American Sociological Review*, Vol. 82, No. 6, 2017, pp. 1167–1187.

Simi, Pete, Steven Windisch, and Karyn Sporer, *Recruitment and Radicalization Among US Far-Right Terrorists*, College Park: National Consortium for the Study of Terrorism and Responses to Terrorism, University of Maryland, November 2016.

Singer, Peter W., and Eric B. Johnson, "The Need to Inoculate Military Servicemembers Against Information Threats: The Case for Digital Literacy Training for the Force," *War on the Rocks*, February 1, 2021. As of February 10, 2021:
https://warontherocks.com/2021/02/we-need-to-inoculate-military-servicemembers-against-information-threats-the-case-for-digital-literacy-training/

Skeem, J., and E. Mulvey, "What Role Does Serious Mental Illness Play in Mass Shootings, and How Should We Address It?" *Criminology and Public Policy*, Vol. 19, No. 1, 2020, pp. 85–108.

Southern Poverty Law Center, "National Alliance," webpage, undated-a. As of March 7, 2021:
https://www.splcenter.org/fighting-hate/extremist-files/group/national-alliance

———, "Neo-Nazi," webpage, undated-b. As of March 7, 2021:
https://www.splcenter.org/fighting-hate/extremist-files/ideology/neo-nazi

Steffens, Maryke S., Adam G. Dunn, Julie Leask, and Kerrie E. Wiley, "How Organisations Promoting Vaccination Respond to Misinformation on Social Media: A Qualitative Investigation," *BMC Public Health*, Vol. 19, No. 1, 2019.

Sweeney, Angela, Beth Filson, Angela Kennedy, Lucie Collinson, and Steve Gillard, "A Paradigm Shift: Relationships in Trauma-Informed Mental Health Services," *BJPsych Advances*, Vol. 24, No. 5, 2018, pp. 319–333.

U.S. Department of Homeland Security, "Snapshot: S&T Develops the First Line of Defense Against Acts of Targeted Violence," August 28, 2018. As of January 19, 2021:
https://www.dhs.gov/science-and-technology/news/2018/08/28/terrorism

Vargas, Briana, and Joel Angel Juarez, "El Pasoans Remember Victims of the Walmart Shooting One Year Later," *Texas Tribune*, August 3, 2020. As of February 5, 2021: https://www.texastribune.org/2020/08/03/el-paso-shooting-anniversary/

Vergani, Matteo, Muhammad Iqbal, Ekin Ilbahar, and Greg Barton, "The Three Ps of Radicalization: Push, Pull and Personal; A Systematic Scoping Review of the Scientific Evidence About Radicalization into Violent Extremism," *Studies in Conflict and Terrorism*, Vol. 43, No. 10, 2020.

Weggemanns, Daan, Edwin Bakker, and Peter Grol, "Who Are They and Why Do They Go? The Radicalisation and Preparatory Processes of Dutch Jihadist Foreign Fighters," *Perspectives on Terrorism*, Vol. 8, No. 4, 2014, pp. 100–110.

Weine, Stevan, and Osman Ahmed, *Building Resilience to Violent Extremism Among Somali-Americans in Minneapolis-St. Paul*, College Park: National Consortium for the Study of Terrorism and Responses to Terrorism, University of Maryland, August 2012.

Weine, Stevan, Schuyler Henderson, Stephen Shanfield, Rupinder Legha, and Jerrold Post, "Building Community Resilience to Counter Violent Extremism," *Democracy and Security*, Vol. 9, No. 4, 2013, pp. 327–333.

Wikipedia, "Heritage Front," webpage, undated. As of March 7, 2021: https://en.wikipedia.org/wiki/Heritage_Front

Williams, Michael J., John G. Horgan, and William P. Evans, "The Critical Role of Friends in Networks for Countering Violent Extremism: Toward a Theory of Vicarious Help-Seeking," *Behavioral Sciences of Terrorism and Political Aggression*, Vol. 8, No. 1, 2016, pp. 45–65.

Windisch, Steven, Gina Scott Ligon, and Pete Simi, "Organizational [Dis]trust: Comparing Disengagement Among Former Left-Wing and Right-Wing Violent Extremists," *Studies in Conflict and Terrorism*, Vol. 42, No. 6, 2019, pp. 559–580.

Wiktorowicz, Quintan, *Islamic Activism: A Social Movement Theory Approach*, Bloomington: Indiana University Press, 2004.

———, *Radical Islam Rising: Muslim Extremism in the West*, Lanham, Md.: Rowman & Littlefield Publishers, 2005.

Wolfowicz, Michael, Yael Litmanovitz, David Weisburd, and Badi Hasisi, "A Field-Wide Systematic Review and Meta-Analysis of Putative Risk and Protective Factors for Radicalization Outcomes," *Journal of Quantitative Criminology*, Vol. 36, 2020, pp. 407–447.

Zmigrod, Leor, Peter Jason Rentfrow, and Trevor W. Robbins, "Cognitive Inflexibility Predicts Extremist Attitudes," *Frontiers in Psychology*, Vol. 10, May 2019.

Zollo, Fabiana, Petra Kralj Novak, Michela Del Vicario, Alessandro Bessi, Igor Mozetič, Antonio Scala, Guido Caldarelli, and Walter Quattrociocchi, "Emotional Dynamics in the Age of Misinformation," *PLoS ONE*, Vol. 10, No. 9, September 2015.